Know Your
Worth

Torn Curtain Publishing
Wellington, New Zealand
www.torncurtainpublishing.com

© Copyright 2021 Ruth Augustine. All rights reserved.

ISBN Softcover 9780645175738

No portion of this book may be reproduced, stored in a retrieval system or transmitted in any form or by any means—electronic, mechanical, photocopy, recording or otherwise—except for brief quotations in printed reviews of promotion, without prior written permission from the author.

All details included in this book are written from the author's best recollection and perspective. This book is not intended as a substitute for professional counselling or medical advice.

Unless otherwise noted, scripture quotations are from the ESV® Bible (The Holy Bible, English Standard Version®), copyright © 2001 by Crossway, a publishing ministry of Good News Publishers. Used by permission. All rights reserved.

Scriptures marked NKJV are taken from the New King James Version®. Copyright © 1982 by Thomas Nelson. Used by permission. All rights reserved.

Cover Art by Emily Ruonala. Used with Permission.
Typeset in Caslon, Oxtail OT, Marydale, P22 Underground

Cataloguing in Publishing Data
Title: Know Your Worth
Author: Ruth Augustine
Subjects: Relationships, Narcissistic abuse, Addiction, Emotional healing, Spiritual Growth

A copy of this title is held at the National Library of Australia.

Know Your
Worth

A Handbook for Emotional Healing

Ruth Augustine

Acknowledgements

My Academy family, the staff and students of 2020 and 2021, thank you. Mark Greenwood, thank you for believing in us, teaching us our righteous identity in Christ, and seeing us the way He does. Mandy and Carston Woodhouse, your prayers and prophecies are what have made this book possible. And Luchi Miranda-Ventura, I don't know how much you are paid but someone needs to double it.

The Overcomers, thank you for constantly calling out the gold in me each week (the best connection group). You made me fearless.

Shu and Andre Longginou, your names have been mentioned throughout this book. You both have blessed me beyond what I have words for. Andre, thank you so much for helping me with the chapter about forgiveness!

Emily Ruonala, thank you for the hours you spent giving me feedback on the original manuscript, and the weeks you spent drafting out the perfect cover art for this book. You are amazing!

Anya McKee, I couldn't have asked for a better coach. A huge thanks to you and your team at Torn Curtain Publishing for making this entire process smooth, easy, and fun.

Michael Gibson, you believe in me more than I believe in myself, and love this book even more than I do. You have been my greatest encouragement and support. Thank you.

It is the Spirit who gives life; the flesh is no help at all. The words that I have spoken to you are spirit and life.

JOHN 6:63

INTRODUCTION

PART ONE

9	Chapter One: **My Testimony**
15	Chapter Two: **God's Mirror**
17	Chapter Three: **Your Words**

PART TWO

23	Chapter Four: **Healing**
29	Chapter Five: **Identity**
43	Chapter Six: **Intimacy**
55	Chapter Seven: **Love**
61	Chapter Eight: **Forgiveness**
69	Chapter Nine: **Rescue**
75	Chapter Ten: **Defence**
89	Chapter Eleven: **Recompense**
96	Chapter Twelve: **Joy**
105	Chapter Thirteen: **Peace**
113	Chapter Fourteen: **Fearlessness**
123	Chapter Fifteen: **Purpose**
131	Chapter Sixteen: **Wisdom**
141	Chapter Seventeen: **Trust**

CONCLUSION

INTRODUCTION

nce upon a time, in a land far, far away, there lived a princess. The princess was a daughter of God Himself. The God who created the sun, the moon, and the stars. God created the princess in His own image, perfectly and intricately. He was intentional about every detail; the mole on her forehead, the colour of her lips, the beautiful way she smiled.

One day, Prince Charming visited the princess's chamber and gifted her with a large mirror. As the princess got ready in front of this mirror each day, she became increasingly frustrated. The lies of the man she once loved were engraved on the top left corner. On the top right were the social media pictures she compared herself to. The mirror began to speak to the princess; it said things like: "you're not enough", "you're too much", "maybe he would have stayed if you had lighter skin or dressed like her", "maybe if you didn't argue so much", "he wouldn't have needed the other girls if you dressed sexier."

Hearing her cry, the princess's father ran to her chamber. His heart was overwhelmed with just one look of her eyes. He too, had bought her a gift. It was a mirror, about the same size as the other one. But on this mirror was engraved the word of God. Words like: "you are altogether beautiful, my love; there is no flaw in you." (Song of Solomon 4:7), and "you are fearfully and wonderfully made" (Psalm 139:14). With this mirror, it was impossible for the princess to see herself without first reading the words of her father. This mirror spoke to her too; it said things like: "you are loved", "you are chosen", "you are accepted."

As the princess spent time gazing at this mirror each day, she discovered her true identity. It changed the way she walked; it changed the way she talked. She gained an inner confidence that couldn't be taken from her. It didn't matter if her phone rang or didn't ring because she was so full of her father's thoughts. The princess's identity became firmly rooted and grounded in what her father wrote about her. Through this mirror, her father gave her a confidence that wasn't dependent on circumstances or what people thought of her. Her father made her whole. He fully satisfied the deepest longings of her heart.

* * *

The Word of God says:

> *For if anyone is a hearer of the word and not a doer, he is like a man* ***who looks intently at his natural face in a mirror****. For he looks at himself and goes away and at once forgets what he was like.*
>
> JAMES 1:23,24

Which mirror are you looking at? Are you seeing yourself through the distorted lens of social media, comparison, or (like me) what your ex may have said about you? Or are you looking in the mirror of the word of God and seeing yourself as He sees you? My prayer is that the word of God becomes the mirror that you behold, so that you see yourself rightly. How your story ends is up to you.

A few months ago, I asked God what He was saying about emotional and narcissistic abuse. I felt Him say, "Women need to know their worth. They are worthy of love and adoration. As they behold Me, they will see their worth. They will see themselves in Me. They will see their beauty in their Creator. They will stop blaming themselves for what they could have done or should have done."

I believe knowing our worth is key. It's very hard to properly love someone if you're struggling to love yourself. And it's very hard to love yourself if you haven't received the love God has for you. When a person perpetrating violence or abuse against their partner knows who they are, and recognises how much value and worth they carry in the eyes of their Heavenly Father, they won't feel the need to control another person. And when a person who is stuck in a cycle of abuse and manipulation recognises their value and worth it will be a lot easier to get out. And that's where healing begins. Hence this book.

27 September 2019

How is it not my fault?

Because he did it to girls in the past. And he'll do it again. Unless he comes to Me and repents. And even I don't have control over that. I've given everyone free will to choose. That's why I've asked you to move away. He does not define your worth or your identity. I know the true desires of your heart. The desires you've buried so deep that you don't even think about anymore. And he's not it.

A toxic relationship may have stripped you of every bit of self-confidence you had. But like the princess in this story, as you spend time gazing into the mirror your Heavenly Father gave you, He will fill you with a supernatural confidence that is not dependent on yourself or on what others think about you, but on Him.

This book is packed with scriptures from the mirror that your Heavenly Father gave you. As you meditate on them, they will act as a healing balm for your soul. Our Father is in the art of beautifying scars. He promises to give us beauty instead of ashes, joy instead of mourning, and praise instead of heaviness (Isaiah 61:3). What the enemy meant for evil, He will use for good (Genesis 50:20; Romans 8:28).

PART ONE

CHAPTER ONE

MY TESTIMONY

The date for our wedding would have been 25 April 2020. It was going to be a destination wedding in Sri Lanka. The bridesmaids would have been in dusty pink, and the groomsmen in dark grey.

When I first met him, he had 'husband material' stamped all over him. He ticked everything on my list of what I wanted in a man—he was a Christian, he was tall, funny, humble, romantic, easy to talk to, hardworking, the list goes on. We had met as children but reconnected online years later after I had moved to another country. For a few months, we messaged each other on social media. When we found out we were both going to be in the same city at the same time, I was excited to see him in person. He turned up with a gift of an expensive pair of shoes. At the time, I didn't think anything of it. He returned to his country soon after, but we talked often by phone and I was excited at the prospect of being in a relationship with him. I desperately wanted to be his girlfriend! When he told me that all his ex-girlfriends cheated on him, and that one of his ex-girlfriends was crazy and controlling, I was drawn to him and believed everything he said.

A few months in, a friend who knew us both called to warn me about him. My friend told me that in the past he had cheated on his ex-girlfriend and gotten another girl pregnant, seeing them both at the same time. When I confronted him, he admitted he had done this. Knowing about his past, and hearing him make excuses, I knew my friend was right—I needed to pull back. But when I tried to amicably end the relationship, he cried and said things that made me feel sorry for him. If anything, he wanted to take our relationship to another level.

It didn't matter what I tried, he wouldn't accept the fact that I wanted to move on from him. I worked at a police station at the time, in their domestic violence unit. One morning, I walked into work and broke down crying. That day, my co-workers told me to write a list of everywhere we had contact; Snapchat, Instagram, Facebook, Messenger, WhatsApp, Gmail. They showed me how to block him on all these apps. Finally, they helped me write a break-up text and block his phone number as well. Although I knew I would miss his friendship, I felt a huge sense of relief and called to thank my friend for saving me from a lot of potential heartache.

Fast forward a week. I am in my bedroom watching YouTube and eating a mango when my ex turns up at my front door. He had flown from another country to see me, bringing with him flowers, chocolate, and a handwritten letter. I felt pursued and, in that moment, he won my heart.

But nothing had changed. He would talk to multiple girls on social media. He would give other girls rides to church and Bible study and intentionally not tell me about it. When I found out about him giving girls rides, I gave him a list of ways we could build trust. One of the ways was for us to share our passwords with each other.

A few weeks later, I had a sick feeling in my stomach and felt the urge to check his social media. I saw that all his messages with his female friends had been deleted. But in his archived messages I found nudes and a video of a girl in a bathtub. It was the same girl he was driving to church and Bible study. In the messages he talked about this girl being his future wife, the best gift ever, and real good at dressing up. When I confronted my boyfriend, he said he was only joking. Again I broke up with him and blocked him, and again he flew over, turned up at my door, and the cycle repeated.

By this point I recognised that my ex was manipulating me. I would Google his behaviour, and videos started coming up on my YouTube recommendations about narcissistic abuse. I watched the videos, read the articles, and was shocked to see the entire relationship laid out like it was textbook. Despite having worked for five years in the domestic violence field, I had never identified my ex's behaviour as abusive because of the love I had for him.

At its best, the relationship was unhealthy. At its worst, it was emotionally abusive. I was unhealthy because I found my worth and security in him. He was unhealthy because he found his worth and security in girls. Throughout our relationship I struggled to trust him. I lost a lot of weight, self-worth, and self-respect. I lost friendships with people who were frustrated with me going back to him. And I began to lose the motivation to live. I experienced suicidal thoughts and often felt the temptation to 'jump' or crash my car. And whenever I tried breaking up with him, he always had the right words to make me stay.

I received many prophetic warnings to get out of the relationship … and trust me, I tried. I tried for almost a year. I changed my phone number, twice. My dad bought me an old Nokia phone that couldn't make international calls or access social media to help me not to contact him. I blocked him on EVERYTHING. I wrote a list titled "Before you unblock him" and kept a copy in my phone, in my wallet, and on my mirror. I took up CrossFit in an attempt to occupy my time. I tried rewarding myself for every day that I didn't speak to him by putting a dollar in a jar. I even saw a counsellor. But nothing worked. I had formed a strong attachment to this man and kept reaching out to him even though the rational part of me didn't want to. I didn't know it at the time, but I had developed a 'trauma bond'—this occurs when the constant push and pull of an abusive relationship has the same addictive effect as a drug. In the end, I prayed that he would break up with me, and eventually he did. This is known as the 'discard phase' of narcissistic abuse.

* * *

My instinct was to try and jump straight into another relationship to stop myself from going back to him. The truth is, I too had insecurities. I constantly felt I needed a man to fill the void. But I was sick of jumping from relationship to relationship. I was desperate for healing. That's when I realised the beautiful ways God was pursuing me. He wanted to heal me more than I wanted to be healed.

During worship at church one evening, my heart ached; I was questioning if my ex's behaviour would have been any different if I were prettier, if I looked or dressed more like one of the other girls he would talk to. That night, a woman I had never met before, prophesied from the stage: "Pretty girl. You. Yes, you!" I turned around, wondering who she was talking to, before realizing it was me. "Pretty girl. You're beautiful!" she said, and continued to prophesy comfort over me.

From that point, I threw myself into church. I began seeing a counsellor and involved myself in a mentorship group that focused on identity. I also enrolled in bible college. The bible college year began with a five-day retreat. During worship at the retreat one evening, I was distracted by how ugly I felt. My skin was darker than everyone else's in the room, but it was exactly the same colour as my ex's. I remembered him telling me how much he hated his dark skin, and realized the other girls he would talk to were all light-skinned. But during worship that night, I had an encounter with God. I felt His eyes gaze at me intently. They looked like flames of fire. He couldn't take His eyes off me. I felt beautiful. I tried to sing, I tried to speak, but I couldn't. I just stood still and watched Him stare at me in adoration. The very next day, about five to seven people told me I was beautiful! I knew it was God speaking to me through them because it only happened that day.

On the night that would have been our wedding, my counsellor, prompted by the Holy Spirit, messaged me only a few minutes before my ex sent me a message. I told her about the text message and she showed me that what he had written was manipulative. My counsellor helped me to stay strong and ignore his message.

After four months of going with no contact, I started to experience bad dreams about my ex. The dreams were about him and other girls, and I would wake up wanting to contact him. Initially the dreams happened once a week, then two to three times a week, and then every night. I felt so weighed down by these dreams. Then, in worship one day, I saw a picture in my mind of me looking at a gigantic rock. The rock represented my problems, including these dreams. I couldn't see past it; it was massive. Suddenly God took me and seated me with Him in Christ in heavenly places (Ephesians 2:6). From where I was seated, I could no longer see the rock. I left that time of worship feeling light and full of joy. God had reminded me that compared to His glory, even trauma and grief are insignificant—and when I reached out to a few people I trusted to pray for me, the dreams stopped.

I was still hurting from my break-up, but during worship at church one evening, God showed me that my heart was actually completely healed and that my mind just needed to match where my heart was. It can take time for your mind to match where your heart is, and the best way to get there is by renewing your mind through the Word of God.

You will have noticed that I have mentioned what happened during worship about five times in this testimony. Most of my encounters of healing with God happened in that place of intimacy with Him. In fact, intimacy with God is the greatest aid to your healing. If you have come out of an abusive relationship, but have nothing or no one better to cling to, it will be extremely hard to stay away and truly break free. But as you allow God to fill that empty void in your heart that longs to be loved, God can and will heal you completely. He promises He is close to the brokenhearted (Psalm 34:18). He heals the brokenhearted and binds up their wounds (Psalm 147:3). Cling to Him, worship Him, and prioritise being in His presence. In His presence there is fullness of joy (Psalm 16:11).

CHAPTER TWO

GOD'S MIRROR

The Hebrew word for 'meditate' is *hâgâ*. *Hâgâ* means to murmur (in pleasure or anger), to ponder, imagine, meditate, mourn, mutter, roar, speak, study, talk, or utter. You can meditate on the scriptures in any way you choose, but one beautiful tool is called lectio divina (Latin for 'holy reading' or 'prayerful reading').

In their book, 'Grasping God's Word, J. Scott Duvall and J. Daniel Hays describe how we can engage in the five phases of lectio divina. They write:

1. SILENCIO (QUIETNESS)

Prepare your heart to hear from God by slowing down. Get settled in one place and begin to quiet yourself before the Lord. As you cast your cares on Him, intentionally begin to let go of the hurry and noise that often prevents us from listening to God. Now is the time to slow down.

2. LECTIO (READING)

Select a passage of scripture and read it slowly and out loud. Forget about reading quickly. Slow down. Use your imagination to picture yourself as part of the setting. Resist the temptation to analyse or judge the text or use the text to develop a message for someone else. Focus on listening as if God were speaking directly to you.

3. MEDITATIO (MEDITATION)

Read the passage again, pausing to let the words sink deeply into your mind and heart. Without trying to over-spiritualise the meaning, ponder what God seems to be saying to you through these words. How does this word or phrase connect with your life right now?

4. ORATIO (PRAYER)

Respond by praying the passage as you read it a third time. Enter into a conversation with God. Honestly and truthfully talk with God about what he seems to be saying to you through this passage. Now is the time to respond to God. How does the passage make you feel? What action or attitude is God calling you to embrace? Respond from your heart to what God is saying.

5. CONTEMPLATIO (CONTEMPLATION)

Rest and wait patiently in the presence of God. As you give God's Spirit time to work in your life, yield to him. Entrust your past, present, and future to the Lord in light of what He has spoken. Ask the Lord to continue to do His transforming work throughout the day as you continue to listen. Conclude with a prayer of thanksgiving.

CHAPTER THREE

YOUR WORDS

Romans 4:17 tells us that God "calls into existence the things that do not exist." Because He created us in His own image (Genesis 1:27), we get to do the same thing! When we speak, we change the future. I saw this firsthand in my family. Even though my dad had all his hair when he was engaged to my mum, he told her, "My dad's bald, you're marrying a bald man." My dad is one of four sons, and guess what? He is the only son who lost his hair!

The words you speak are extremely powerful! In fact, Proverbs 18:21 says:

> *Death and life are in the power of the tongue,*
> *and those who love it will eat its fruits.*

In the notes section of my phone I have compiled a list of declarations under headings like: "My relationship with God", "My family", "My job", "My friends", "My dreams", "Me", "My husband". I love to declare what I want to see happen in my life! I have many testimonies of what God has done through the words I have declared over my life. When I was unemployed and looking for a job, I would declare everything I wanted in a job. Three months later, I was blessed with a job that completely aligned with what I declared! When I was praying for friends I would declare, "I have lots of Christian friends that I go on adventures with." God brought Christian friends into my life who invited me salsa dancing, stand up paddle boarding, and mountain climbing. I would also declare, "People are drawn to me." I later found out that someone actually prayed they could be my friend!

At the end of each section of scriptures in this book are declarations that you can speak over your life. If you have a sick feeling in the pit of your stomach, go to the section of this book called *God's Mirror Words about Peace* and speak those declarations out loud. If your ex is making up lies about you, go to the section called *God's Mirror Words about Recompense* and declare "Instead of my shame I will have double honor" (Isaiah 61:7 NKJV). When you need to remind yourself of your identity and worth, go to the *God's Mirror Words about Identity* section of this book and speak life over yourself. It won't be long before you start to enjoy the fruit of your words.

***

Lately in my 'alone time' with God I have been reading through the book of Proverbs and re-writing every verse that speaks about the power of our words into the back of my journal. Because I recognise how powerful my words are, I want to be more intentional with how I use them. One morning Proverbs 4:23 (NKJV) was highlighted to me. It says:

> *Keep your heart with all diligence, for out of it*
> *spring the issues of life.*

I was then led to Luke 6:45:

> The good person out of the good treasure of his heart produces good, and the evil person out of his evil treasures produces evil, for out of the abundance of the heart his mouth speaks.

As I was meditating on these verses, I saw an image in my mind of a water-filtering jug. The filter on the jug represented the Word of God. I felt God say, "Don't focus so much on what comes out of your mouth. Focus more on what gets into your heart. Use a water filter."

We must guard and protect our mind, will and emotions because what fills our mind is what will come out of our mouth, and what comes out of our mouth will determine the direction of our lives. In Psalm 141 David prayed:

> Set a guard, O Lord, over my mouth; keep watch over the door of my lips! Do not let my heart incline to any evil, to busy myself with wicked deeds in company with men who work iniquity, and let me not eat of their delicacies! (vv. 3 & 4).

What goes in must come out. So consider: Who do you spend your time with? What do you listen to? What do you watch? James 3:10-12 says:

> From the same mouth come blessing and cursing. My brothers, these things ought not to be so. Does a spring pour forth from the same opening both fresh and salt water? Can a fig tree, my brothers, bear olives, or a grapevine produce figs? Neither can a salt pond yield fresh water.

Filter what goes into your heart, because what you take in will determine what comes out of your mouth. Your words have the power to change everything. In the next section, you will find scriptures and declarations that you can speak over your life, along with powerful activations that will help you break free of the past, and step confidently into your future.

PART TWO

CHAPTER FOUR

HEALING

A few months ago, a teacher at the bible college I attend shared a powerful perspective about divine healing. He said that our healing is actually included in what Jesus achieved on the cross (the atonement). In other words, when Jesus died and rose again, He paid for not only our salvation but also for our healing.

Isaiah 53:4-5 says:

> *Surely he has borne our griefs and carried our sorrows; yet we esteemed him stricken, smitten by God, and afflicted. But he was pierced for our transgressions; he was crushed for our iniquities; upon him was the chastisement that brought us peace, and with his wounds we are healed.*

The Hebrew word for 'griefs' is *hălîy*, which means malady, anxiety, calamity, disease, grief, and sickness.

The Hebrew word for 'sorrows' is *mak'ôb*, which means anguish, affliction, grief, pain (pain physically and pain mentally), and sorrow.

In the exact same way that Jesus carried our sin on the cross, He carried our anxiety, grief, and pain. And in the exact same way Jesus purchased our salvation on the cross, He purchased our emotional, mental and physical healing.

ACTIVATION

Choose a verse from the following scriptures about healing to meditate on using the five phases of lectio divina.

GOD'S MIRROR WORDS ABOUT HEALING

He heals the brokenhearted and binds up their wounds.

PSALM 147:3

Surely he has borne our griefs and carried our sorrows; yet we esteemed him stricken, smitten by God, and afflicted. But he was pierced for our transgressions; he was crushed for our iniquities; upon him was the chastisement that brought us peace, and with his wounds we are healed.

ISAIAH 53:4-5

The Spirit of the Lord God is upon me, because the Lord has anointed me to bring good news to the poor; he has sent me to bind up the brokenhearted, to proclaim liberty to the captives, and the opening of the prison to those who are bound; to proclaim the year of the Lord's favor, and the day of vengeance of our God; to comfort all who mourn; to grant to those who mourn in Zion – to give them a beautiful headdress instead of ashes, the oil of gladness instead of mourning, the garment of praise instead of a faint spirit; that they may be called oaks of righteousness, the planting of the Lord, that he may be glorified.

ISAIAH 61:1-3

For to us a child is born, to us a son is given; and the government shall be upon his shoulder, and his name shall be called Wonderful Counselor, Mighty God, Everlasting Father, Prince of Peace.

ISAIAH 9:6

The Lord is near to the brokenhearted and saves the crushed in spirit.

PSALM 34:18

Then they cried to the Lord in their trouble, and he delivered them from their distress. He sent out his word and healed them, and delivered them from their destruction.

PSALM 107:19-20

Blessed be the God and Father of our Lord Jesus Christ, the Father of mercies and God of all comfort, who comforts us in all our affliction, so that we may be able to comfort those who are in any affliction, with the comfort with which we ourselves are comforted by God.

2 CORINTHIANS 1:3-4

He himself bore our sins in his body on the tree, that we might die to sin and live to righteousness. By his wounds you have been healed. For you were straying like sheep, but have now returned to the Shepherd and Overseer of your souls.

1 PETER 2:24-25

Therefore, confess your sins to one another and pray for one another, that you may be healed. The prayer of a righteous person has great power as it is working. Elijah was a man with a nature like ours, and he prayed fervently that it might not rain, and for three years and six months it did not rain on the earth.

JAMES 5:16-17

O Lord my God, I cried to you for help, and you have healed me.

PSALM 30:2

Blessed are those who mourn, for they shall be comforted.

MATTHEW 5:4

For I will restore health to you, and your wounds I will heal, declares the Lord, because they have called you an outcast: 'It is Zion, for whom no one cares!'

JEREMIAH 30:17

I DECLARE:

God has healed my broken heart, healed my wounds, and restored health to me. (Psalm 147:3; Jeremiah 30:17)

By Jesus' wounds I am healed. (Isaiah 53:4-5; 1 Peter 2:24-25)

God has given me beauty instead of ashes, exceeding joy instead of mourning, and praise instead of heaviness. (Isaiah 61:1-3)

The Lord is close to me. (Psalm 34:18)

Jesus is my Wonderful Counselor, Mighty God, Everlasting Father, and Prince of Peace. He is the Shepherd and Overseer of my soul. (Isaiah 9:6; 1 Peter 2:24-25)

God sent out his word and healed me. He delivered me from my distress and destruction. (Psalm 107:19-20)

I am comforted by God himself; the God of all comfort, who comforts me, so that I can comfort others. (Matthew 5:4, 2 Corinthians 1:3-4)

CHAPTER FIVE

IDENTITY

It was a Monday morning when I received a stream of text messages from my ex that brought me to tears. Thankfully, Monday mornings are when we have corporate worship at my bible college, and our time of worship made me feel a lot better. At lunch time I walked past a girl called Shu, who I didn't know very well at the time. I smiled and said "hi", and she asked me if I wanted to have lunch with her. As I sat down, she began to prophesy over me regarding my identity. Here's what she said:

> "I see this really vivid vision in my mind that before you were born, when you were still in your mother's womb, God was so excited. I felt Him saying, 'I'm going to host the biggest celebration for my girl's life!' I also saw Him design a whole chamber for you by Himself. He built this chamber for you with His own hands. When you were born, He was so excited to just linger and examine you for hours. And now you've become a woman, so I see that every morning when you wake up there are a few angels

around you brushing your hair and putting these very expensive oils, fragrances, and spices on your skin, to look after you and to dress you up for the day. I see God running toward your chamber saying, 'I heard that my girl is waking up, I can't wait to see her!' He's running toward you saying, 'Wow you're so beautiful, you're so precious, you're so wonderful. You're perfect, you're really perfect in my sight.'"

She then continued:

"What I also feel, is that you are not a beggar with dirt on your face saying, 'Oh please give me some love, some cheap love.' No! You are literally the princess that God has hidden in your chamber for so long."

Over lunch, Shu continued to prophesy about how God is examining His sons' hearts to pick the best one for me, His girl. Shu said that because God adores me so much, He wants someone who loves me in the same way He loves me. "God is already working," she said. "I'm saying to you that He's working! His heart is so *for you!*"

I recorded Shu's prophecy on my phone and listened to it every day for weeks. As I relistened to it today to type into this book, I could hear myself crying in the background. It has only been six months since I received that prophecy, and I genuinely cannot recognise the girl I was back then. When God shows you your worth, begging for cheap love is completely out of character.

How God feels about me is the exact same way He feels about you. You are not a beggar on the street crying out for cheap love. You are a child of God. Your worth doesn't come from anyone else. Your worth comes from the Creator of heaven, of earth, and of you. Gaze into God's mirror to see who you are, and let how He feels about you speak louder than how your ex made you feel about yourself.

SUNFLOWERS AND ROSES

In my dream last night, I saw two different girls about to get married. Let's call them Candace and Janice. When Candace saw that Janice got her wedding dress from the same designer as her, she angrily tore a part of Janice's wedding dress. Janice fought back, ruining Candace's wedding dress as well. In my dream, I sat with Candace and told her what I want to tell you: *Another girl's beauty doesn't take away yours.*

In the dream, I asked Candace what her favourite type of flower was. She wasn't sure. I then told her that you can't compare a sunflower with a rose; they are completely different but both are beautiful. In the same way, you can't compare yourself with anyone else. Another girl's beauty doesn't take away from your own. You can't compare a sunflower with a rose. You can't compare a packet of Maltesers with a Snickers bar. You can't compare yourself with the girl he cheated on you with. You don't need to put her down to bring yourself up. You're already up! You were handmade by the same designer—your Heavenly Father. You weren't bought at an op shop. Nothing about you is secondhand. One design may be different to the other, but His designs are never outdated; they never go out of style. There's beauty in every dress. Another girl's beauty doesn't take away yours. You don't need to put on makeup. You don't need to take off your clothes. You can just be you and that's more than enough.

AN EVER-CHANGING STANDARD

I'm learning to stop being so obsessed about my body. I used to weigh myself every single day, count my calories, and train my glutes about four times a week. I literally found a photo of my dream body, photoshopped my face on it, and stuck it on my bedroom wall.

A few weeks ago, as I woke up, God reminded me, "You are altogether beautiful, my love; there is no flaw in you." (Song of Solomon 4:7). "Every *body* is different," He said. "It doesn't need to be perfect. What is perfection anyway? It's an ever-changing standard."

In my mind I saw an image of a bar that represented my goal weight. When I reached it, the bar was raised to a lower weight. I jumped and reached that too, so the bar was raised again. Pretty quickly the bar was too high for me to reach, so I needed a stool. The stool represented surgeries, lip injections, butt injections . . . the bar kept being lifted higher until I jumped and fell off the stool. I felt God say, "See, it's an ever-changing standard. You'll kill yourself trying to reach it."

You were hand made by the Creator of the universe. His fingerprints are all over your body. You were intricately woven in your mother's womb. He made you, chose you, accepted you, before you had even heard of Him. He loved you. Deeply. He chose your skin colour. He could have made you any colour, but He chose this one for you. God doesn't make ugly. All His creation is beautiful. When He formed you, He was intentional about every detail. He was purposeful.

He is pleased with you! You're His child. You're His beloved. You're perfect in His sight. I'm not just saying this out of 'faith'—it's true, and I'm confident of it. He knew the problems you would face and the mistakes you would make, and He made you anyway. He was excited about you. And He still is. If He could change anything about you, He wouldn't. He could change anything about you, and He chose not to. His eyes are on you constantly. He has waited for you. He loves you, unconditionally. He didn't love you more back then. And He didn't love you less. He'll never love you more than He does in this moment. He has washed you clean.

- Reject the lie that you're not worthy.
- Reject the lie that you're inadequate.
- Reject the lie that there's something wrong with you.
- Reject the lie that you're rejected!

Ask your Heavenly Father to show you the truth. The truth is, you're beautiful. You radiate God's beauty. You are a child of the most high God. He is pleased with you. He is certain of you. He's not an indecisive God. He doesn't get it wrong.

ACTIVATION

Psalm 85:8 says:

Let me hear what God the Lord will speak for He will speak peace to His people, to His saints; but let them not turn back to folly.

Sit with God and identify any lies that you are believing about yourself. Ask God what the truth is and without overthinking or filtering anything write down what you feel He is saying. If you feel to, write down what He says on sticky notes and stick them on the mirror you use every day.

GOD'S MIRROR WORDS ABOUT IDENTITY

But to all who did receive him, who believed in his name, he gave the right to become children of God, who were born, not of blood nor of the will of the flesh nor of the will of man, but of God.

JOHN 1:12-13

For you did not receive the spirit of slavery to fall back into fear, but you have received the Spirit of adoption as sons, by whom we cry, "Abba! Father!"

ROMANS 8:15

Before I formed you in the womb I knew you, and before you were born I consecrated you; I appointed you a prophet to the nations.

JEREMIAH 1:5

For you formed my inward parts; you knitted me together in my mother's womb. I praise you, for I am fearfully and wonderfully made. Wonderful are your works; my soul knows it very well. My frame was not hidden from you, when I was being made in secret, intricately woven in the depths of the earth.

PSALM 139:13-15

Your eyes saw my unformed substance; in your book were written, every one of them, the days that were formed for me, when as yet there was none of them.

PSALM 139:16

But who are you, O man, to answer back to God? Will what is molded say to its molder, "Why have you made me like this?"

ROMANS 9:20

But now, O Lord, you are our Father; we are the clay, and you are our potter; we are all the work of your hand.

ISAIAH 64:8

For we are his workmanship, created in Christ Jesus for good works, which God prepared beforehand, that we should walk in them.

EPHESIANS 2:10

You are altogether beautiful, my love; there is no flaw in you.

SONG OF SOLOMON 4:7

Not that we dare to classify or compare ourselves with some of those who are commending themselves. But when they measure themselves by one another and compare themselves with one another, they are without understanding.

2 CORINTHIANS 10:12

He found him in a desert land, and in the howling waste of the wilderness; he encircled him, he cared for him, he kept him as the apple of his eye. Like an eagle that stirs up its nest, that flutters over its young, spreading out its wings, catching them, bearing them on its pinions, the Lord alone guided him, no foreign god was with him.

DEUTERONOMY 32:10-12

Can a woman forget her nursing child, that she should have no compassion on the son of her womb? Even these may forget, yet I will not forget you. Behold, I have engraved you on the palms of my hands; your walls are continually before me.

ISAIAH 49:15–16

Are not two sparrows sold for a penny? And not one of them will fall to the ground apart from your Father. But even the hairs of your head are all numbered. Fear not, therefore; you are of more value than many sparrows.

MATTHEW 10:29–31

How precious to me are your thoughts, O God! How vast is the sum of them! If I would count them, they are more than the sand. I awake, and I am still with you.

PSALM 139:17–18

For our sake he made him to be sin who knew no sin, so that in him we might become the righteousness of God.

2 CORINTHIANS 5:21

But you are a chosen race, a royal priesthood, a holy nation, a people for his own possession, that you may proclaim the excellencies of him who called you out of darkness into his marvelous light.

1 PETER 2:9

You were bought with a price; do not become bondservants of men.

1 CORINTHIANS 7:23

You are the light of the world. A city set on a hill cannot be hidden. Nor do people light a lamp and put it under a basket, but on a stand, and it gives light to all in the house. In the same way, let your light shine before others, so that they may see your good works and give glory to your Father who is in heaven.

MATTHEW 5:14-16

What is man that you are mindful of him, and the son of man that you care for him? Yet you have made him a little lower than the heavenly beings and crowned him with glory and honor.

PSALM 8:4-5

You did not choose me, but I chose you and appointed you that you should go and bear fruit and that your fruit should abide, so that whatever you ask the Father in my name, he may give it to you.

JOHN 15:16

I have been crucified with Christ. It is no longer I who live, but Christ who lives in me. And the life I now live in the flesh I live by faith in the Son of God, who loved me and gave himself for me.

GALATIANS 2:20

The Spirit himself bears witness with our spirit that we are children of God, and if children, then heirs – heirs of God and fellow heirs with Christ, provided we suffer with him in order that we may also be glorified with him.

ROMANS 8:16-17

Or do you not know that your body is a temple of the Holy Spirit within you, whom you have from God? You are not your own, for you were bought with a price. So glorify God in your body.

I CORINTHIANS 6:19-20

For you are a people holy to the Lord your God, and the Lord has chosen you to be a people for his treasured possession, out of all the peoples who are on the face of the earth.

DEUTERONOMY 14:2

The wicked flee when no one pursues, but the righteous are bold as a lion.

PROVERBS 28:1

By this is love perfected with us, so that we may have confidence for the day of judgment, because as he is so also are we in this world.

I JOHN 4:17

But God, being rich in mercy, because of the great love with which he loved us, even when we were dead in our trespasses, made us alive together with Christ – by grace you have been saved – and raised us up with him and seated us with him in the heavenly places in Christ Jesus, so that in the coming ages he might show the immeasurable riches of his grace in kindness toward us in Christ Jesus.

EPHESIANS 2:4-7

In him we live and move and have our being; as even some of your own poets have said, 'For we are indeed his offspring.'

ACTS 17:28

Whoever believes in me, as the Scripture has said, 'Out of his heart will flow rivers of living water.'

JOHN 7:38

And these signs will accompany those who believe: in my name they will cast out demons; they will speak in new tongues; they will pick up serpents with their hands; and if they drink any deadly poison, it will not hurt them; they will lay their hands on the sick, and they will recover.

MARK 16:17-18

Whoever confesses that Jesus is the Son of God, God abides in him, and he in God.

I JOHN 4:15

For if anyone is a hearer of the word and not a doer, he is like a man who looks intently at his natural face in a mirror. For he looks at himself and goes away and at once forgets what he was like. But the one who looks into the perfect law, the law of liberty, and perseveres, being no hearer who forgets but a doer who acts, he will be blessed in his doing.

JAMES 1:23-25

I Declare:

I am a child of God. I was born of God. (John 1:12-13, Romans 8:15)

Before God formed me in the womb he knew me, and before I was born he consecrated me. (Jeremiah 1:5)

God formed my inward parts; he knit me together in my mother's womb. I am fearfully and wonderfully made. God's works are wonderful; my soul knows it very well. My frame was not hidden from him, when I was being made in secret, intricately woven in the depths of the earth. (Psalm 139:13-15)

God's eyes saw my unformed substance; in his book were written the days that were formed for me, when there was none of them. (Psalm 139:16)

I am God's workmanship, created in Christ Jesus for good works, which God prepared beforehand, that I should walk in them. (Ephesians 2:10)

I am altogether beautiful; there is no flaw in me. (Song of Solomon 4:7)

I don't compare myself to anyone else. (2 Corinthians 10:12)

God has kept me as the apple of his eye. (Deuteronomy 32:10-12)

God has engraved me on the palms of his hands. (Isaiah 49:15-16)

Even the hairs of my head are all numbered. (Matthew 10:29-31)

God's thoughts toward me outnumber the sand. (Psalm 139:17-18)

I am chosen, royal, and holy. I am God's treasured possession. God called me out of darkness into his marvelous light. (Deuteronomy 14:2, 1 Peter 2:9)

I was bought with a price. (1 Corinthians 7:23)

God has crowned me with glory and honor. (Psalm 8:4-5)

Whatever I ask the Father in Jesus' name, he gives to me. (John 15:16)

I have been crucified with Christ. It is no longer I who live, but Christ who lives in me. (Galatians 2:20)

I am the righteousness of God in Christ. (2 Corinthians 5:21)

I am as bold as a lion. (Proverbs 28:1)

As Jesus is, so am I in this world. (1 John 4:17)

I am the light of the world. (Matthew 5:14-16)

I am a coheir with Christ. (Romans 8:16-17)

I am seated with God in the heavenly places in Christ Jesus. (Ephesians 2:4-7)

In him I live and move and have my being. (Acts 17:28)

Rivers of living water flow out of my heart. (John 7:38)

In Jesus' name I cast out demons; speak in new tongues; and lay hands on the sick and see them recover. If I drink any deadly poison, it will not hurt me. (Mark 16:17-18)

My body is a temple of the Holy Spirit within me. I am not my own. God abides in me, and I in God. (1 Corinthians 6:19-20, 1 John 4:15)

The word of God is my mirror, and it reminds me of who I am. (James 1:23-24)

CHAPTER SIX

INTIMACY

I was looking forward to Saturday. I had kept my entire weekend free to spend time with God. I had my Bible, journal, and worship music ready. Saturday morning came, and I woke up feeling rejected. I ignored the feeling and spent time with God anyway. Turning on my worship music, I closed my eyes, and sang along. About an hour later, I was disappointed. I still felt rejected and ended up numbing my pain by scrolling through social media. The feeling of rejection carried into the next day. I moved from my bed to my couch but repeated the numbing process by scrolling once again.

Hours later I went back to my bedroom, threw myself on my bed and said, "God I feel rejected!" Then, He spoke. I wrote down His words to me:

9 August 2020

It wasn't rejection, Ruthie. I pulled him out of your life. Nothing about that was rejection. He didn't have the

> character to sustain a long-term relationship with you. Nothing about that was your fault. There is nothing you could have done to change the outcome. It was I who brought separation. I am a protective Father.

In that minute, God shifted my entire perspective. Rejection left, and joy came.

Lamentations 2:19 says,

> *Pour out your heart like water before the presence of the Lord!*

John 4:23 says,

> *The true worshipers will worship the Father in spirit and truth, for the Father is seeking such people to worship him.*

God loves it when we are real with Him. My most effective prayer that weekend was, "God I feel rejected!" If you are concerned you can't hear God's voice, let me assure you that you can. John 10:26-27 says,

> *You do not believe because you are not among my sheep. My sheep hear my voice, and I know them, and they follow me.*

If you believe in Jesus, you are among His sheep. And His sheep hear His voice. God speaks in different ways. He might show you a picture in your mind. He might remind you of a song. He might prompt you to turn to a particular Bible verse. He might give you a dream. He might softly whisper to your heart. Steward what He tells you by keeping a record of what He says. He will shift your entire perspective.

ACTIVATION

Get comfortable. Grab your Bible, journal, and favourite drink. Turn on some worship music if you like. Begin spending time with God with a prayer of thanksgiving. Psalm 100:4 says:

> *Enter His gates with thanksgiving, and His courts with praise! Give thanks to Him; bless His name!*

Then, pour out your heart like water before the presence of the Lord (Lamentations 2:19) and be completely honest with Him about how you feel and what you need. He is the greatest comforter.

God's Mirror Words About Intimacy

Behold, I stand at the door and knock. If anyone hears my voice and opens the door, I will come in to him and eat with him, and he with me.

REVELATION 3:20

As an apple tree among the trees of the forest, so is my beloved among the young men. With great delight I sat in his shadow, and his fruit was sweet to my taste.

SONG OF SOLOMON 2:3

Come, everyone who thirsts, come to the waters; and he who has no money, come, buy and eat! Come, buy wine and milk without money and without price. Why do you spend your money for that which is not bread, and your labor for that which does not satisfy? Listen diligently to me, and eat what is good, and delight yourselves in rich food.

ISAIAH 55:1-2

Jesus said to her, "Everyone who drinks of this water will be thirsty again, but whoever drinks of the water that I will give him will never be thirsty again. The water that I will give him will become in him a spring of water welling up to eternal life."

JOHN 4:13-14

For with you is the fountain of life; in your light do we see light.

PSALM 36:7-9

The sun shall be no more your light by day, nor for brightness shall the moon give you light; but the Lord will be your everlasting light, and your God will be your glory. Your sun shall no more go down, nor your moon withdraw itself; for the Lord will be your everlasting light, and your days of mourning shall be ended.

ISAIAH 60:19-20

As for me, I shall behold your face in righteousness; when I awake, I shall be satisfied with your likeness.

PSALM 17:15

For he satisfies the longing soul, and the hungry soul he fills with good things.

PSALM 107:9

The Lord is my shepherd; I shall not want. He makes me lie down in green pastures. He leads me beside still waters. He restores my soul. He leads me in paths of righteousness for his name's sake.

PSALM 23:1-3

How precious is your steadfast love, O God! The children of mankind take refuge in the shadow of your wings. They feast on the abundance of your house, and you give them drink from the river of your delights. By day the Lord commands his steadfast love, and at night his song is with me, a prayer to the God of my life.

PSALM 42:8

Your word is a lamp to my feet and a light to my path.

PSALM 119:105

Bless the Lord, O my soul, and all that is within me, bless his holy name! Bless the Lord, O my soul, and forget not all his benefits, who forgives all your iniquity, who heals all your diseases, who redeems your life from the pit, who crowns you with steadfast love and mercy, who satisfies you with good so that your youth is renewed like the eagle's. The Lord works righteousness and justice for all who are oppressed.

PSALM 103:1-6

I bless the Lord who gives me counsel; in the night also my heart instructs me.

PSALM 16:7

If you love me, you will keep my commandments. And I will ask the Father, and he will give you another Helper, to be with you forever, even the Spirit of truth, whom the world cannot receive, because it neither sees him nor knows him. You know him, for he dwells with you and will be in you.

JOHN 14:15-17

Abide in me, and I in you. As the branch cannot bear fruit by itself, unless it abides in the vine, neither can you, unless you abide in me.

JOHN 15:4

This Book of the Law shall not depart from your mouth, but you shall meditate on it day and night, so that you may be careful to do according to all that is written in it. For then you will make your way prosperous, and then you will have good success.

JOSHUA 1:8

But the fruit of the Spirit is love, joy, peace, patience, kindness, goodness, faithfulness, gentleness, self-control; against such things there is no law.

GALATIANS 5:22-23

Nevertheless, I am continually with you; you hold my right hand.

PSALM 73:23

Likewise the Spirit helps us in our weakness. For we do not know what to pray for as we ought, but the Spirit himself intercedes for us with groanings too deep for words. And he who searches hearts knows what is the mind of the Spirit, because the Spirit intercedes for the saints according to the will of God.

ROMANS 8:26-27

For we do not have a high priest who is unable to sympathize with our weaknesses, but one who in every respect has been tempted as we are, yet without sin. Let us then with confidence draw near to the throne of grace, that we may receive mercy and find grace to help in time of need.

HEBREWS 4:15-16

And this is the confidence that we have toward him, that if we ask anything according to his will he hears us. And if we know that he hears us in whatever we ask, we know that we have the requests that we have asked of him.

I JOHN 5:14-15

So Jesus said to the Jews who had believed him, "If you abide in my word, you are truly my disciples, and you will know the truth, and the truth will set you free."

JOHN 8:31-32

Before I was afflicted I went astray, but now I keep your word. You are good and do good; teach me your statutes.

PSALM 119:67-68

Do not be conformed to this world, but be transformed by the renewal of your mind, that by testing you may discern what is the will of God, what is good and acceptable and perfect.

ROMANS 12:2

My sheep hear my voice, and I know them, and they follow me. I give them eternal life, and they will never perish, and no one will snatch them out of my hand.

JOHN 10:27-28

Call to me and I will answer you, and I will tell you great and hidden things that you have not known.

JEREMIAH 33:3

Whom have I in heaven but you? And there is nothing on earth that I desire besides you. My flesh and my heart may fail, but God is the strength of my heart and my portion forever.

PSALM 73:25-26

His mouth is most sweet, and he is altogether desirable. This is my beloved and this is my friend, O daughters of Jerusalem.

SONG OF SOLOMON 5:16

Lord, you hear the desire of the afflicted; you will strengthen their heart; you will incline your ear to do justice to the fatherless and the oppressed, so that man who is of the earth may strike terror no more.

PSALM 10:17–18

For God alone, O my soul, wait in silence, for my hope is from him. He only is my rock and my salvation, my fortress; I shall not be shaken.

PSALM 62:5-6

Blessed are those who dwell in your house, ever singing your praise! Blessed are those whose strength is in you, in whose heart are the highways to Zion. As they go through the Valley of Baca they make it a place of springs; the early rain also covers it with pools. They go from strength to strength; each one appears before God in Zion.

PSALM 84:4–7

He who dwells in the shelter of the Most High will abide in the shadow of the Almighty. I will say to the Lord, "My refuge and my fortress, my God, in whom I trust."

PSALM 91:1-2

He will cover you with his pinions, and under his wings you will find refuge; his faithfulness is a shield and buckler.

PSALM 91:4

The young lions suffer want and hunger; but those who seek the Lord lack no good thing.

PSALM 34:10

Delight yourself in the Lord, and he will give you the desires of your heart.

PSALM 37:4

If you abide in me, and my words abide in you, ask whatever you wish, and it will be done for you.

JOHN 15:7

Ask, and it will be given to you; seek, and you will find; knock, and it will be opened to you. For everyone who asks receives, and the one who seeks finds, and to the one who knocks it will be opened. Or which of you, if his son asks him for bread, will give him a stone? Or if he asks for a fish, will give him a serpent? If you then, who are evil, know how to give good gifts to your children, how much more will your Father who is in heaven give good things to those who ask him!

MATTHEW 7:7-11

I DECLARE:

God satisfies my soul and fills it with good things. (Psalm 107:9)

Because I drink of the water that Jesus gives me, I will never be thirsty again. (John 4:13-14)

The Lord is my everlasting light and glory. The days of my mourning are over. (Isaiah 60:19-20)

The Lord is my shepherd; I shall not want. He makes me lie down in green pastures. He leads me beside still waters. He restores my soul. He leads me in paths of righteousness for his name's sake. (Psalm 23:1-3)

The Lord heals me, redeems me, and crowns me with love. The Lord works justice for me. (Psalm 103:1-6)

God has given me a Helper, the Spirit of truth. I know him, because he dwells with me and is in me. (John 14:15-17)

I have all the fruit of the Spirit; love, joy, peace, patience, kindness, goodness, faithfulness, gentleness, and self-control. (Galatians 5:22-23)

The Holy Spirit helps me in my weakness. When I pray in tongues, the Holy Spirit intercedes for me according to the will of God. (Romans 8:26-27)

I abide in God's word. I know the truth, and the truth has set me free. (John 8:31-32)

I hear God's voice, and I follow him. No one will snatch me out of God's hand. (John 10:27-28)

When I call to God, he answers me, and tells me great and hidden things. (Jeremiah 33:3)

God is continually with me; he holds my right hand. (Psalm 73:23)

There is nothing on earth that I desire besides God. God is the strength of my heart and my portion forever. (Psalm 73:25-26)

As I go through the valley of weeping I make it a place of springs. I go from strength to strength. (Psalm 84:4-7)

God is my refuge and my fortress. (Psalm 91:1-2)

God's faithfulness is my shield. (Psalm 91:4)

Because I seek the Lord I lack no good thing. (Psalm 34:10)

I delight myself in the Lord, and he gives me the desires of my heart. (Psalm 37:4)

CHAPTER SEVEN

LOVE

I can relate to the Samaritan woman who had five husbands and was living with her sixth man (see John 4). I had tried to fill the God-sized void in my heart with validation from boys. My worth and value was dependent on whether a boy liked me or not. Although I was raised in a Christian home, only recently have I discovered the love I have been looking for my entire life: Jesus.

About three months after my break up, during an encounter with God, I felt Jesus show me that this, my relationship with Him, is the main event ... the main meal. Marriage is not going to save me. I've already found the main thing. He is what I was waiting for all along. Not marriage.

I got free from finding my security in relationships, but quickly started finding my security in friendships instead. During worship at our college's end-of-year retreat, I saw an image of me standing on top of a hill. The outer layer of the hill was made of clay, and the foundation underneath was a large rock. The clay represented those I was placing my security in—my friends. The rock represented Jesus. The clay began to shake, and God took the clay away so I could stand on the solid, unshakable rock—Jesus. God then handed me flowers, which represented my friends. I felt God say to me that night, "Insecurity is just finding security in the wrong thing."

A boyfriend, marriage, friends—they are all beautiful things. But if we stand on them for our security, rather than holding them like beautiful flowers, we will remain insecure. Our security must be found in Jesus and Jesus alone.

The day I found out my boyfriend had been giving girls rides and intentionally not telling me about it, I had woken up with Isaiah 54:10 on my heart:

> *For the mountains may depart and the hills' be removed,*
> *but my steadfast love shall not depart from you, and my covenant of*
> *peace shall not be removed,' says the Lord, who has compassion on you.*

Everything you stood on for security may have left you, or been taken from you. But God's enduring love will never leave you, and His promise of peace will never be taken away. God can fill the void in you that makes you feel like something is missing. He can satisfy it better than anyone else. He knows your deepest desires, the longings you have put aside and almost forgotten. He knows your desire to be loved. He is more real than you think.

ACTIVATION

In your time with God, ask Him the following questions: *Am I worth fighting for? Do you cherish me? Am I lovely?* (These questions were the same questions my counsellor encouraged me to ask God after our first counselling session, and they were inspired by the book Captivating by John and Stasi Eldredge.)

God's Mirror Words About Love

No, in all these things we are more than conquerors through him who loved us. For I am sure that neither death nor life, nor angels nor rulers, nor things present nor things to come, nor powers, nor height nor depth, nor anything else in all creation, will be able to separate us from the love of God in Christ Jesus our Lord.

ROMANS 8:37-39

My beloved speaks and says to me: "Arise, my love, my beautiful one, and come away, for behold, the winter is past; the rain is over and gone. The flowers appear on the earth, the time of singing has come, and the voice of the turtledove is heard in our land. The fig tree ripens its figs, and the vines are in blossom; they give forth fragrance. Arise, my love, my beautiful one, and come away. O my dove, in the clefts of the rock, in the crannies of the cliff, let me see your face, let me hear your voice, for your voice is sweet, and your face is lovely."

SONG OF SOLOMON 2:10-14

She shall pursue her lovers but not overtake them, and she shall seek them but shall not find them. Then she shall say, 'I will go and return to my first husband, for it was better for me then than now.' And she did not know that it was I who gave her the grain, the wine, and the oil, and who lavished on her silver and gold, which they used for Baal. Therefore I will take back my grain in its time, and my wine in its season, and I will take away my wool and my flax, which were to cover her nakedness.

HOSEA 2:7-9

Therefore, behold, I will allure her, and bring her into the wilderness, and speak tenderly to her. And there I will give her vineyards and make the Valley of Achor a door of hope. And there shall she answer as in the days of her youth, as at the time when she came out of the land of Egypt.

HOSEA 2:14-15

And I will betroth you to me forever. I will betroth you to me in righteousness and in justice, in steadfast love and in mercy. I will betroth you to me in faithfulness. And you shall know the Lord.

HOSEA 2:19-20

For this reason I bow my knees before the Father, from whom every family in heaven and on earth is named, that according to the riches of his glory he may grant you to be strengthened with power through his Spirit in your inner being, so that Christ may dwell in your hearts through faith — that you, being rooted and grounded in love, may have strength to comprehend with all the saints what is the breadth and length and height and depth, and to know the love of Christ that surpasses knowledge, that you may be filled with all the fullness of God. Now to him who is able to do far more abundantly than all that we ask or think, according to the power at work within us, to him be glory in the church and in Christ Jesus throughout all generations, forever and ever. Amen.

EPHESIANS 3:14-21

Behold, you are beautiful, my love; behold, you are beautiful; your eyes are doves.

SONG OF SOLOMON 1:15

As a lily among brambles, so is my love among the young women.

SONG OF SOLOMON 2:2

He brought me to the banqueting house, and his banner over me was love.

SONG OF SOLOMON 2:4

You have captivated my heart, my sister, my bride; you have captivated my heart with one glance of your eyes, with one jewel of your necklace. How beautiful is your love, my sister, my bride! How much better is your love than wine, and the fragrance of your oils than any spice!

SONG OF SOLOMON 4:9-10

Turn away your eyes from me, for they overwhelm me — Your hair is like a flock of goats leaping down the slopes of Gilead.

SONG OF SOLOMON 6:5

How beautiful and pleasant you are, O loved one, with all your delights!

SONG OF SOLOMON 7:6

I am my beloved's and my beloved is mine; he grazes among the lilies.

SONG OF SOLOMON 6:3

For the Lord takes pleasure in his people; he adorns the humble with salvation.

PSALM 149:4

The Lord your God is in your midst, a mighty one who will save; he will rejoice over you with gladness; he will quiet you by his love; he will exult over you with loud singing.

ZEPHANIAH 3:17

There is no fear in love, but perfect love casts out fear. For fear has to do with punishment, and whoever fears has not been perfected in love. We love because he first loved us.

I JOHN 4:18-19

I Declare:

I am more than a conqueror through God who loves me. (Romans 8:37)

Nothing and no one can separate me from the love of God. (Romans 8:38-39)

God is pursuing me. He longs to see my face and hear my voice. (Song of Solomon 2:10-14)

I have captivated God's heart with one glance of my eyes. (Song of Solomon 4:9)

My eyes overwhelm the Lord. (Song of Solomon 6:5)

I am beautiful and a pleasure to love. (Song of Solomon 1:15; Song of Solomon 7:6)

I have doves eyes. (Song of Solomon 1:15)

God's banner over me is love. (Song of Solomon 2:4)

God rejoices over me with gladness and singing, He quietens me with his love. (Zephaniah 3:17)

God's perfect love for me casts out all fear. (1 John 4:18-19)

I am rooted and grounded in love. I comprehend the love of God that surpasses knowledge. I am filled with the fullness of God. God is able to do far more abundantly than all that I ask or think according to the power at work within me. (Ephesians 3:14-21)

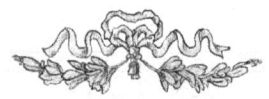

CHAPTER EIGHT

FORGIVENESS

Unforgiveness is like drinking poison yourself and waiting for the other person to die.

I'm not going to sit here and pretend I know what you have been through. I honestly don't know what you have been through. Only you and God know the amount of pain you have experienced. Only you and God know the rejection you feel, the betrayal you went through, and the confusion that is lingering. And if you have felt stuck in an emotionally abusive relationship for any period of time, you are probably used to forgiving your ex.

When I went through my breakup, the last thing I wanted to read about was forgiveness. I would feel encouraged by inspirational quotes about my worth but quickly scroll straight past anything about forgiveness because I didn't want to risk going back to my ex. Half the reason I went back to him as many times as I did was because I kept forgiving him. "Love believes the best", right? But forgiveness doesn't always mean reconciliation. I'll address this more towards the end of this book.

While I don't know what you have been through, what I do know, is that forgiveness is essential to your healing. Again, I am not telling you to contact your ex and tell him you have forgiven him. In fact, I am definitely not telling you to do that! I am a strong advocate of the block and delete button. But if you had a wound on your knee and it still had dirt in it, what would you do? You would cleanse it so that the wound could heal. It's the same with an emotional wound. The wound is cleaned by the process of forgiveness. Forgiveness does not mean going back to an abusive relationship, but it does mean the letting go of anger, bitterness and resentment. This gives the Jesus, our Physician the chance to heal the wound.

Imagine your soul as a garden where you and the Holy Spirit get to walk together, pruning and pulling out weeds, and planting new beautiful trees and flowers. When you identify something poisonous, you need to address it immediately. Stewardship of our heart is incredibly important, because everything flows from this place, whether good or bad, and it will reveal what is within. As Proverbs 4:23 (AMP) says,

Watch over your heart with all diligence, for from it flow the springs of life.

I never wanted to become a bitter, man-hating woman, still angry about an ex from years ago. My prayer has always been that God would use the pain I experienced to restore me to something even better than I was before. He has done that. And He can do the same for you.

ACTIVATION

Firstly, forgive your ex of every wrong-doing, and be detailed:

> *Father I forgive (ex's name) for rejecting me and leaving me for someone else.*
>
> *Father I forgive (ex's name) for lying to me and manipulating me.*

Forgive yourself for your past mistakes too.

> *I forgive myself for making that mistake.*

Ask God for forgiveness through repentance (this means to do a complete 180-degree turn away from doing that again, toward the direction of living God's way).

> *Father please forgive me. I repent of the mistake of (be specific).*

Then honestly bless your ex with all your heart, ask God to free them. Whether they meant to harm you or not, they need God's help!

> *Father please have mercy on (ex's name).*
>
> *I bless (ex's name) in Jesus' name and ask that you would draw him closer to you and show him how you see him.*

Then ask God to heal you, and receive it by faith. Picture the dirt in your imagination cleaned out of the wound.

> *Father please heal my wounds, and make me stronger than ever.*

Every time you get a painful memory of the past flash before you, repeat this process until one day it stops because it's completely healed.

God's Mirror Words About Forgiveness

Be angry and do not sin; do not let the sun go down on your anger, and give no opportunity to the devil.

EPHESIANS 4:26-27

Be angry, and do not sin; ponder in your own hearts on your beds, and be silent. Selah.

PSALM 4:4

Let all bitterness and wrath and anger and clamor and slander be put away from you, along with all malice.

EPHESIANS 4:31

For if you forgive others their trespasses, your heavenly Father will also forgive you, but if you do not forgive others their trespasses, neither will your Father forgive your trespasses.

MATTHEW 6:14-15

For as high as the heavens are above the earth, so great is his steadfast love toward those who fear him; as far as the east is from the west, so far does he remove our transgressions from us.

PSALM 103:11-12

I, I am he who blots out your transgressions for my own sake, and I will not remember your sins.

ISAIAH 43:25

Bless those who persecute you; bless and do not curse them.

ROMANS 12:14

You have heard that it was said, 'You shall love your neighbor and hate your enemy.' But I say to you, Love your enemies and pray for those who persecute you, so that you may be sons of your Father who is in heaven. For he makes his sun rise on the evil and on the good, and sends rain on the just and on the unjust. For if you love those who love you, what reward do you have? Do not even the tax collectors do the same? And if you greet only your brothers, what more are you doing than others? Do not even the Gentiles do the same? You therefore must be perfect, as your heavenly Father is perfect.

MATTHEW 5:43-48

Do not be overcome by evil, but overcome evil with good.

ROMANS 12:21

I Declare:

I let go of all bitterness, anger, and malice. (Ephesians 4:31)

I forgive my ex and all who have hurt me. (Matthew 6:14-15)

I am forgiven. God does not remember my sins. (Isaiah 43:25)

I bless those who persecute me; I bless and do not curse them. (Romans 12:14)

I love my enemies and pray for those who persecute me. (Matthew 5:43–48)

I am not overcome by evil, I overcome evil with good. (Romans 12:21)

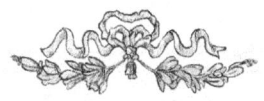

CHAPTER NINE
RESCUE

Many times during my struggle to break free from my relationship with my ex, I would ask God for a sign. I knew without any doubt that God didn't want me to be in that relationship! And yet, I kept asking God for a sign because I desperately wanted to be with him. My ex promised me that he had changed, and I wanted so badly to believe him. I had made an idol out of the relationship and was willing to compromise in my relationship with God just to stay with him.

One particular morning as I walked into church I said in my mind, "God, show me a sign about him". After the service that morning, a man at my church approached me and said that he wanted to talk to me before I left. When we spoke, I was shocked at the accuracy of the prophetic words he gave me. He said he saw an image of me leaning against a large oak tree which was giving me shade and security. He said that the oak tree had a love carving on it, and it was as though I was in love with someone and was waiting for something to happen. He then said that God was asking me to walk away from that oak tree because there was nothing there anymore. "It's just memories now", he said. He also said that the relationship was affecting my health, and he was right. He had noticed that I lost a lot of weight and that he couldn't recognise me when I walked into church because of how much weight I had lost. I cried and asked him, "How?!" How was I meant to walk away? I knew that I wasn't meant to be in that relationship but I didn't know how to get out and stay out. He told me that he would pray for me, and that was that.

I discovered later that the 'how' to getting out and staying out, was found in intimacy with God, and being in community with others. Intimacy with God and community with others is what showed me my worth, and knowing my worth enabled me to never look back.

ACTIVATION

Go to the *I declare* section of this chapter and read the declarations out loud.

GOD'S MIRROR WORDS ABOUT RESCUE

I called on your name, O Lord, from the depths of the pit; you heard my plea, 'Do not close your ear to my cry for help!' You came near when I called on you; you said, 'Do not fear!'
LAMENTATIONS 3:55-57

I waited patiently for the Lord; he inclined to me and heard my cry. He drew me up from the pit of destruction, out of the miry bog, and set my feet upon a rock, making my steps secure. He put a new song in my mouth, a song of praise to our God. Many will see and fear, and put their trust in the Lord.
PSALM 40:1-3

He sets on high those who are lowly, and those who mourn are lifted to safety.
JOB 5:11

When I thought, "My foot slips," your steadfast love, O Lord, held me up.
PSALM 94:18

My eyes are ever toward the Lord, for he will pluck my feet out of the net.
PSALM 25:15

The Lord preserves the simple; when I was brought low, he saved me. Return, O my soul, to your rest; for the Lord has dealt bountifully with you. For you have delivered my soul from death, my eyes from tears, my feet from stumbling; I will walk before the Lord in the land of the living.

PSALM 116:6-9

I Declare:

God heard my cry. He drew me up from the pit of destruction, and set my feet upon a rock, making my steps secure. God put a new song in my mouth, a song of praise. Many will see and fear, and put their trust in the Lord. (Psalm 40:1-3)

God sets me on high, and lifts me to safety. (Job 5:11)

God's steadfast love holds me up. (Psalm 94:18)

My eyes are fixed on God, because he plucks my feet out of the net. (Psalm 25:15)

When I was brought low, God saved me. My soul rests. He has delivered my soul from death, my eyes from tears, my feet from stumbling. (Psalm 116:6-9)

CHAPTER TEN

DEFENCE

The princess listened to the crunching sound of the autumn leaves under her feet as she went for her morning walk through the woods. Each crunch felt like a massage for her mind which seemed to be constantly racing. As she approached the open field, a group of armed men and women began to taunt her. Prince Charming, along with his new partner and his friends, encircled her, armed with bows and arrows. In unison they shot at her, each arrow piercing a different part of her body. The princess tried to defend herself, but an arrow pierced her eye, and in a moment, she lost her sight.

Her father ran to her defence. He covered her with a shield (Psalm 5:12). He gently took the arrow out of her eye; He healed her sight. He prepared a table for her, in the presence of her enemies (Psalm 23:5). The princess fixed her eyes on her father's, and ate every word that came out of his mouth. He served her an abundance of love, joy, and peace. He gave her a beautiful pair of diamond earrings that represented a double recompense.

The diamonds shone so bright it was impossible for anybody to look at the princess without noticing the double recompense on her ears. The princess's focus changed from fighting her enemies to fulfilling the call her father had on her life.

***

When God is your defender, you don't need to defend yourself. If your ex is making up lies about you, if mutual friends suddenly stop talking to you, you don't need to justify yourself. You don't need to prove yourself to anyone. You don't need to prove your worth to anyone. Not everyone is going to see your worth, just as not everyone sees God's. Isaiah 54:17 says, "No weapon formed against you will prosper". Psalm 23:5 says that God will prepare a table for you in the presence of your enemies.

If your vision of how you see yourself has been tainted by the words spoken against you, God will heal your eyes and help you see yourself as He sees you. He will never waste your pain. Instead of your shame, He will give you double honor (Isaiah 61:7). Your reputation is in God's hands. Let them lie. God is your defender. God is your vindicator. God is your advocate.

When I felt that lies were being told about me, I received a prophetic word by a friend who didn't know what was happening in my life at the time. He said, "It is the Lord who defends you. He is with you in everything. He is your advocate. When the enemy accuses you of anything, Jesus steps in front and is that barricade. He's a good lawyer. He's the best lawyer in town. You can stand fully assured that you are justified, washed, free to reign, explore, and just be you. The angel of the Lord encamps around those who fear Him (Psalm 34:7)."

ACTIVATION

When Jesus was being tempted by the devil in the wilderness, He spoke the word of God (Matthew 4:1-11). He would say, "It is written", and quote the Bible. There is power in speaking scripture. Psalm 103:20 says that angels obey the voice of God's word. Go through the verses in this book, or in your Bible, and choose 8-10 verses you can say out loud everyday. Write them somewhere handy, and when the enemy comes against you with fiery darts, say these scriptures out loud. Say them as often as you can. The verses on my personal list are:

Proverbs 28:1; Galatians 2:20; 2 Timothy 1:7, 12; 2 Timothy 2:4; Psalm 5:12; Isaiah 54:17; Isaiah 41:10.

God's Mirror Words About Defence

In righteousness you shall be established; you shall be far from oppression, for you shall not fear; and from terror, for it shall not come near you. If anyone stirs up strife, it is not from me; whoever stirs up strife with you shall fall because of you.

ISAIAH 54:14-15

No weapon that is fashioned against you shall succeed, and you shall refute every tongue that rises against you in judgment. This is the heritage of the servants of the Lord and their vindication is from me, declares the Lord.

ISAIAH 54:17

You, O Lord, are a shield about me, my glory, and the lifter of my head.

PSALM 3:3

The Lord will fight for you, and you have only to be silent.

EXODUS 14:14

Beloved, never avenge yourselves, but leave it to the wrath of God, for it is written, "Vengeance is mine, I will repay, says the Lord."

ROMANS 12:19

When a man's ways please the Lord, he makes even his enemies to be at peace with him.

PROVERBS 16:7

You have kept count of my tossings; put my tears in your bottle. Are they not in your book? Then my enemies will turn back in the day when I call. This I know, that God is for me. In God, whose word I praise, in the Lord, whose word I praise, in God I trust; I shall not be afraid. What can man do to me?

PSALM 56:8-11

The Lord will cause your enemies who rise against you to be defeated before you. They shall come out against you one way and flee before you seven ways.

DEUTERONOMY 28:7

Do not say, "I will repay evil"; wait for the Lord, and he will deliver you.

PROVERBS 20:22

A false witness will not go unpunished, and he who breathes out lies will not escape.

PROVERBS 19:5

Say to those who have an anxious heart, "Be strong; fear not! Behold, your God will come with vengeance, with the recompense of God. He will come and save you."

ISAIAH 35:4

But the Lord is faithful. He will establish you and guard you against the evil one.

2 THESSALONIANS 3:3

I, I am he who comforts you; who are you that you are afraid of man who dies, of the son of man who is made like grass, and have forgotten the Lord, your Maker, who stretched out the heavens and laid the foundations of the earth, and you fear continually all the day because of the wrath of the oppressor, when he sets himself to destroy? And where is the wrath of the oppressor? He who is bowed down shall speedily be released; he shall not die and go down to the pit, neither shall his bread be lacking. I am the Lord your God, who stirs up the sea so that its waves roar – the Lord of hosts is his name.

ISAIAH 51:12-15

Out of my distress I called on the Lord; the Lord answered me and set me free. The Lord is on my side; I will not fear. What can man do to me?

PSALM 118:5-6

What then shall we say to these things? If God is for us, who can be against us? He who did not spare his own Son but gave him up for us all, how will he not also with him graciously give us all things? Who shall bring any charge against God's elect? It is God who justifies. Who is to condemn? Christ Jesus is the one who died – more than that, who was raised – who is at the right hand of God, who indeed is interceding for us.

ROMANS 8:31-34

Show me a sign of your favor, that those who hate me may see and be put to shame because you, Lord, have helped me and comforted me.

PSALM 86:17

If it had not been for the Lord who was on our side when people rose up against us, then they would have swallowed us up alive, when their anger was kindled against us; then the flood would have swept us away, the torrent would have gone over us; then over us would have gone the raging waters. Blessed be the Lord who has not given us as prey to their teeth! We have escaped like a bird from the snare of the fowlers; the snare is broken, and we have escaped! Our help is in the name of the Lord, who made heaven and earth.

PSALM 124:2-8

You shall seek those who contend with you, but you shall not find them; those who war against you shall be as nothing at all. For I, the Lord your God, hold your right hand; it is I who say to you, "Fear not, I am the one who helps you."

ISAIAH 41:12-13

Finally, be strong in the Lord and in the strength of his might. Put on the whole armor of God, that you may be able to stand against the schemes of the devil. For we do not wrestle against flesh and blood, but against the rulers, against the authorities, against the cosmic powers over this present darkness, against the spiritual forces of evil in the heavenly places. Therefore take up the whole armor of God, that you may be able to withstand in the evil day, and having done all, to stand firm. Stand therefore, having fastened on the belt of truth, and having put on the breastplate of righteousness, and, as shoes for your feet, having put on the readiness given by the gospel of peace. In all circumstances take up the shield of faith, with which you can extinguish all the flaming darts of the evil one; and take the helmet of salvation, and the sword of the Spirit, which is the word of God.

EPHESIANS 6:10-17

Evening and morning and at noon I utter my complaint and moan, and he hears my voice. He redeems my soul in safety from the battle that I wage, for many are arrayed against me. God will give ear and humble them, he who is enthroned from of old, because they do not change and do not fear God. My companion stretched out his hands against his friends; he violated his covenant. His speech was smooth as butter, yet war was in his heart; his words were softer than oil, yet they were drawn swords. Cast your burden on the Lord and he will sustain you; he will never permit the righteous to be moved.

PSALM 55:18-22

Though an army encamp against me, my heart shall not fear; though war arise against me, yet I will be confident. One thing have I asked of the Lord, that will I seek after: that I may dwell in the house of the Lord all the days of my life, to gaze upon the beauty of the Lord and to inquire in his temple. For he will hide me in his shelter in the day of trouble; he will conceal me under the cover of his tent; he will lift me high upon a rock. And now my head shall be lifted up above my enemies all around me, and I will offer in his tent sacrifices with shouts of joy; I will sing and make melody to the Lord.

PSALM 27:3-6

He sent from on high, he took me; he drew me out of many waters. He rescued me from my strong enemy and from those who hated me, for they were too mighty for me. They confronted me in the day of my calamity, but the Lord was my support. He brought me out into a broad place; he rescued me, because he delighted in me.

PSALM 18:16-19

Because you have made the Lord your dwelling place – the Most High, who is my refuge – no evil shall be allowed to befall you, no plague come near your tent. For He will command his angels concerning you to guard you in all your ways. On their hands they will bear you up, lest you strike your foot against a stone. You will tread on the lion and the adder; the young lion and the serpent you will trample underfoot. Because he holds fast to me in love, I will deliver him; I will protect him, because he knows my name. When he calls to me, I will answer him; I will be with him in trouble; I will rescue him and honor him.

PSALM 91:9-15

I lift up my eyes to the hills. From where does my help come? My help comes from the Lord, who made heaven and earth. He will not let your foot be moved; he who keeps you will not slumber. Behold, he who keeps Israel will neither slumber nor sleep. The Lord is your keeper; the Lord is your shade on your right hand. The sun shall not strike you by day, nor the moon by night. The Lord will keep you from all evil; he will keep your life. The Lord will keep your going out and your coming in from this time forth and forevermore.

PSALM 121:1-8

The Lord lives, and blessed be my rock, and exalted be the God of my salvation – the God who gave me vengeance and subdued peoples under me, who rescued me from my enemies; yes, you exalted me above those who rose against me; you delivered me from the man of violence.

PSALM 18:46-48

Teach me your way, O Lord, and lead me on a level path because of my enemies. Give me not up to the will of my adversaries; for false witnesses have risen against me, and they breathe out violence.

PSALM 27:11–12

I will extol you, O Lord, for you have drawn me up and have not let my foes rejoice over me.

PSALM 30:1

A thousand may fall at your side, ten thousand at your right hand, but it will not come near you. You will only look with your eyes and see the recompense of the wicked.

PSALM 91:7–8

Blessed are you when others revile you and persecute you and utter all kinds of evil against you falsely on my account. Rejoice and be glad, for your reward is great in heaven, for so they persecuted the prophets who were before you.

MATTHEW 5:11–12

Let not those rejoice over me who are wrongfully my foes, and let not those wink the eye who hate me without cause. For they do not speak peace, but against those who are quiet in the land they devise words of deceit. They open wide their mouths against me; they say, "Aha, Aha! Our eyes have seen it!" You have seen, O Lord; be not silent! O Lord, be not far from me! Awake and rouse yourself for my vindication, for my cause, my God and my Lord! Vindicate me, O Lord, my God, according to your righteousness, and let them not rejoice over me!

PSALM 35:19–24

Be not silent, O God of my praise! For wicked and deceitful mouths are opened against me, speaking against me with lying tongues. They encircle me with words of hate, and attack me without cause. In return for my love they accuse me, but I give myself to prayer.

PSALM 109:1-4

They band together against the life of the righteous and condemn the innocent to death. But the Lord has become my stronghold, and my God the rock of my refuge.

PSALM 94:21-22

Submit yourselves therefore to God. Resist the devil, and he will flee from you.

JAMES 4:7

Those who seek my life lay their snares; those who seek my hurt speak of ruin and meditate treachery all day long. But I am like a deaf man; I do not hear, like a mute man who does not open his mouth. I have become like a man who does not hear, and in whose mouth are no rebukes. But for you, O Lord, do I wait; it is you, O Lord my God, who will answer.

PSALM 38:12-15

I am weary with my moaning; every night I flood my bed with tears; I drench my couch with my weeping. My eye wastes away because of grief; it grows week because of all my foes. Depart from me, all you workers of evil, for the Lord has heard my plea; the Lord accepts my prayer.

PSALM 6:6-9

I Declare:

I am established in righteousness; I am far from oppression, because I do not fear; and from terror, because it does not come near me. (Isaiah 54:14-15)

No weapon formed against me will prosper. (Isaiah 54:17)

God is my shield, my glory, and the lifter of my head. (Psalm 3:3)

The Lord is fighting for me, and I only need to be silent. (Exodus 14:14)

Vengeance is the Lord's, he will repay. (Romans 12:19)

The Lord is faithful. He will establish me and guard me against the evil one. (2 Thessalonians 3:3)

Out of my distress I called on the Lord; the Lord answered me and set me free. The Lord is on my side; I will not fear. What can man do to me? (Psalm 118:5-6)

If God is for me, who can be against me? It is God who justifies. Christ Jesus is at the right hand of God interceding for me. (Romans 8:31-34)

I cast my burden on the Lord and he sustains me. (Psalm 55:18-22)

I resist the devil, and he flees from me. (James 4:7)

My heart does not fear; I am confident. The one thing that I seek after is to dwell in the house of the Lord all the days of my life, to gaze upon his beauty, and inquire in his temple. He hides me in his shelter in the day of trouble; he lifts me high upon a rock. (Psalm 27:3-6)

My help is in the name of the Lord, who made heaven and earth. (Psalm 124:2-8)

A thousand may fall at my side, ten thousand at my right hand, but it will not come near me. (Psalm 91:7-8)

Because I have made the Lord my dwelling place – the Most High, who is my refuge – no evil is allowed to come near me. God commands his angels to guard me in all my ways. God delivers me, protects me, answers me, rescues me, and honors me. (Psalm 91:9-15)

The Lord is my keeper. The Lord keeps me from all evil; he keeps my life. (Psalm 121)

Because my ways please the Lord, he makes even my enemies to be at peace with me. (Proverbs 16:7)

I am strong in the Lord. I put on the whole armor of God. I put on the belt of truth, the breastplate of righteousness, and the helmet of salvation. As shoes for my feet, I put on the readiness given by the gospel of peace. I pick up the shield of faith and the sword of the Spirit, which is the word of God. (Ephesians 6:10-17)

CHAPTER ELEVEN

RECOMPENSE

Gary Chapman describes five "love languages", or ways we give and receive love. These are: words of affirmation, acts of service, gifts, quality time, and physical touch. Personally, my love languages are words of affirmation and physical touch. Understandably, I am obsessed with handwritten letters—they're words that you can touch! When my ex and I were together, I used to jokingly-but-seriously ask him to send me letters. I remember pulling into my driveway and glancing over at my letterbox with the secret hope that there might be a letter from him. But he never really sent me any letters. Fast forward to when we finally broke up . . . heaps of people started writing me letters, people who had no idea what I was going through! One letter was left on my car, another posted to my address, and many letters were handed to me in person. For my birthday, my connection group from the bible college gave me a jar of letters! I started pinning these letters on my bedroom wall, but it got to the point where it would look messy if I put them all up there because of how many letters I was getting!

Isaiah 61:7 says,

> *Instead of your shame you shall have double honor, and instead of confusion they shall rejoice in their portion. Therefore in their land they shall possess double; everlasting joy shall be theirs.*

We get to sow every shameful experience and reap a harvest of double honour. Let me translate that for you: You are going to have twice as much honour just because of the shameful experience you have been through. I am confident that I now enjoy 'double honour' because of what I went through with my ex. One of my prayers while I was still healing was that I would come out better than I was before. That I would be better than I would have been had I not gone through what I went through. And I can honestly say that is what happened. Romans 8:28 says,

> *And we know that for those who love God all things work together for good, for those who are called according to his purpose.*

God is not going to waste your pain. He's going to give you double honour. He promised.

ACTIVATION

Re-write Isaiah 61:7 at the top of a new page in your journal. Bonus points if you re-write this verse using your own words. Beneath this verse, write out every shameful experience you would like to exchange for a double recompense. For example, if you lost a lot of confidence because of your relationship, give that to God and thank Him in advance for restoring double the confidence you lost. You'll look back at this list and praise Him for His faithfulness!

GOD'S MIRROR WORDS ABOUT RECOMPENSE

Instead of your shame you shall have double honor, and instead of confusion they shall rejoice in their portion. Therefore in their land they shall possess double; everlasting joy shall be theirs.

ISAIAH 61:7 NKJV

And we know that for those who love God all things work together for good, for those who are called according to his purpose.

ROMANS 8:28

As for you, you meant evil against me, but God meant it for good, to bring it about that many people should be kept alive, as they are today.

GENESIS 50:20

The thief comes only to steal and kill and destroy. I came that they may have life and have it abundantly.

JOHN 10:10

You prepare a table before me in the presence of my enemies; you anoint my head with oil; my cup overflows.

PSALM 23:5

For who is God, but the Lord? And who is a rock, except our God? – the God who equipped me with strength and made my way blameless. He made my feet like the feet of a deer and set me secure on the heights.

PSALM 18:31-33

Surely goodness and mercy shall follow me all the days of my life, and I shall dwell in the house of the Lord forever.

PSALM 23:6

But, as it is written, "What no eye has seen, nor ear heard, nor the heart of man imagined, what God has prepared for those who love him."

I CORINTHIANS 2:9

You have given me the shield of your salvation, and your right hand supported me, and your gentleness made me great. You gave a wide place for my steps under me, and my feet did not slip.

PSALM 18:35-36

Behold, the former things have come to pass, and new things I now declare; before they spring forth I tell you of them.

ISAIAH 42:9

Remember not the former things, nor consider the things of old. Behold, I am doing a new thing; now it springs forth, do you not perceive it? I will make a way in the wilderness and rivers in the desert.

ISAIAH 43:18-19

Arise, shine, for your light has come, and the glory of the Lord has risen upon you. For behold, darkness shall cover the earth, and thick darkness the peoples; but the Lord will arise upon you, and his glory will be seen upon you.

ISAIAH 60:1-2

Strength and dignity are her clothing, and she laughs at the time to come.

PROVERBS 31:25

The Lord upholds all who are falling and raises up all who are bowed down. The eyes of all look to you, and you give them their food in due season. You open your hand; you satisfy the desire of every living thing.

PSALM 145:14-16

Humble yourselves, therefore, under the mighty hand of God so that at the proper time he may exalt you, casting all your anxieties on him, because he cares for you.

I PETER 5:6-7

Humble yourselves before the Lord, and he will exalt you.

JAMES 4:10

But the path of the righteous is like the light of dawn, which shines brighter and brighter until full day.

PROVERBS 4:18

Before destruction a man's heart is haughty, but humility comes before honor.

PROVERBS 18:12

For it is you who light my lamp; the Lord my God lightens my darkness.

PSALM 18:2

I DECLARE:

Instead of my shame I will have double honor, instead of confusion I will rejoice in my portion. Everlasting joy is mine. (Isaiah 61:7)

God is working all things together for good. (Romans 8:28)

God came that I may have life and have it abundantly. (John 10:10)

God is preparing a table before me in the presence of my enemies. (Psalm 23:5)

Goodness and mercy follow me every day. (Psalm 23:6)

My path is like the light of dawn, which shines brighter and brighter until full day. (Proverbs 4:18)

I don't remember the former things, I don't consider the things of old. God is doing a new thing; now it springs forth. God is making a way in the wilderness and rivers in the desert. (Isaiah 42:9; Isaiah 43:18-19)

Strength and dignity are my clothing, and I laugh at the time to come. (Proverbs 31:25)

I humble myself under the mighty hand of God and at the proper time he will exalt me. I cast all my anxieties on him, because he cares for me. (1 Peter 5:6-7; James 4:10)

God has equipped me with strength and made my way blameless. (Psalm 18:31-33)

God has given me the shield of his salvation, and his right hand supports me, and his gentleness makes me great. (Psalm 18:35-36)

The Lord upholds me, raises me up, and satisfies my desires. (Psalm 145:14-16)

I am not prideful but I am humble, therefore I recieve honour. (Proverbs 18:12)

I shine because my light has come, and the glory of the Lord is seen on me. (Isaiah 60:1-2)

The Lord my God lightens my darkness. (Psalm 18:28)

CHAPTER TWELVE

JOY

If your happiness was in a bowl, who would be holding it? Your ex or you? If your ex is holding your bowl of happiness, they have the ability to take from it, put more into it, or even drop it. When you give your bowl to someone else, two things can happen—you give another person either too much power, or too much pressure. Either you give them the power to make or break you, or you place them under pressure to keep you happy.

The only person responsible for your bowl of happiness is you. But do you know what is even better than holding your own bowl of happiness? Letting Jesus hold it. When you let Jesus carry your bowl, He'll take care of it better than you can. He'll protect it more than you can. And it won't even be a bowl anymore! It will be an abundant, limitless supply.

Psalm 16:11 says:

> *You make known to me the path of life; in your presence there is fullness of joy; at your right hand are pleasures forevermore.*

Don't give anyone else the power to make or break you. Don't even give yourself that amount of pressure. Take the power back, take the pressure off, and give your bowl to Jesus. Jesus is the best person to carry your bowl of happiness. When we go to Him for our happiness, He takes our heartache and replaces it with joy. Isaiah 61:3 says He gives us beauty for ashes, joy for mourning, and praise instead of heaviness. In His presence you will experience the fullness of joy that God has for you (Psalm 16:11).

ACTIVATION

Psalm 16:11 says in God's presence there is fullness of joy. A beautiful way to experience God's presence is through worship. Worship helps us take our eyes off ourselves and puts them on the Father. I encourage you to put on some worship music, sing along, dance along, and worship your Father.

Another practical activation you can do is create a joy plan. Write a list of everything that brings you joy and then add them into your daily routine. Here was mine:

4 December 2019

My joy plan:

- *Focus on intimacy with Jesus – stay FULL of God.*
- *Control what you surround yourself with– take a break from social media until at least Christmas*
- *Thank God everyday– 10 new things*
- *Dance*
- *Read*

— Do CrossFit 3x per week

— Stop telling everyone over and over what happened

— When thoughts about him come up- pray for him and take negative thoughts captive (replace them with the word of God- "the prudent man sees the evil and hides himself", "instead of my former shame I shall have a twofold recompense", "God's peace and completeness will not be removed from me")

God's Mirror Words About Joy

You have loved righteousness and hated wickedness; therefore God, your God, has anointed you with the oil of gladness beyond your companions.

HEBREWS 1:9

You make known to me the path of life; in your presence there is fullness of joy; at your right hand are pleasures forevermore.

PSALM 16:11

For His anger is but for a moment, His favor is for a life; Weeping may endure for a night, but joy comes in the morning.

PSALM 30:5 (NKJV)

Then shall the young women rejoice in the dance, and the young men and the old shall be merry. I will turn their mourning into joy; I will comfort them, and give them gladness for sorrow. I will feast the soul of the priests with abundance, and my people shall be satisfied with my goodness, declares the Lord.

JEREMIAH 31:13-14

But let all who take refuge in you rejoice; let them ever sing for joy, and spread your protection over them, that those who love your name may exult in you. For you bless the righteous, O Lord; you cover him with favor as with a shield.

PSALM 5:11-12

Those who sow in tears shall reap with shouts of joy!

PSALM 126:5

Rejoice in the Lord always; again I will say, rejoice.

PHILIPPIANS 4:4

A joyful heart is good medicine, but a crushed spirit dries up the bones.

PROVERBS 17:22

All the days of the afflicted are evil, but the cheerful of heart has a continual feast.

PROVERBS 15:15

This is the day that the Lord has made; let us rejoice and be glad in it.

PSALM 118:24

Not only that, but we rejoice in our sufferings, knowing that suffering produces endurance, and endurance produces character, and character produces hope, and hope does not put us to shame, because God's love has been poured into our hearts through the Holy Spirit who has been given to us.

ROMANS 5:3–5

Count it all joy, my brothers, when you meet trials of various kinds, for you know that the testing of your faith produces steadfastness. And let steadfastness have its full effect, that you may be perfect and complete, lacking nothing.

JAMES 1:2–4

But he said to me, "My grace is sufficient for you, for my power is made perfect in weakness." Therefore I will boast all the more gladly of my weaknesses, so that the power of Christ may rest upon me. For the sake of Christ, then, I am content with weaknesses, insults, hardships, persecutions, and calamities. For when I am weak, then I am strong.

2 CORINTHIANS 12:9-10

Rejoice always, pray without ceasing, give thanks in all circumstances; for this is the will of God in Christ Jesus for you.

1 THESSALONIANS 5:16-18

You have turned for me my mourning into dancing; you have loosed my sackcloth and clothed me with gladness, that my glory may sing your praise and not be silent. O Lord my God, I will give thanks to you forever!

PSALM 30:11-12

I will greatly rejoice in the Lord; my soul shall exult in my God, for he has clothed me with the garments of salvation; he has covered me with the robe of righteousness, as a bridegroom decks himself like a priest with a beautiful headdress, and a bride adorns herself with her jewels.

ISAIAH 61:10

I will rejoice and be glad in your steadfast love, because you have seen my affliction; you have known the distress of my soul, and you have not delivered me into the hand of the enemy; you have set my feet in a broad place.

PSALM 31:7-8

I Declare:

Because I love righteousness and hate wickedness; God has anointed me with exceeding joy beyond my companions. (Hebrews 1:9)

In God's presence there is fullness of joy. (Psalm 16:11)

Because I have sown in tears, I will reap with shouts of joy! (Psalm 126:5)

My weeping may last for the night, but joy comes in the morning. (Psalm 30:5)

God has turned my mourning into joy; he comforts me and gives me gladness for sorrow. (Jeremiah 31:13-14)

I rejoice always, pray without ceasing, and give thanks in all circumstances. (1 Thessalonians 5:16-18)

I have a joyful heart. (Proverbs 17:22; Proverbs 15:15)

This is the day that the Lord has made; I will rejoice and be glad in it. (Psalm 118:24)

I rejoice in my sufferings; knowing that suffering produces endurance, and endurance produces character, and character produces hope, and hope does not put me to shame, because God's love has been poured into my heart through the Holy Spirit who has been given to me. (Romans 5:3-5)

God's grace is enough for me, his power is made perfect in weakness. (2 Corinthians 12:9-10)

God spreads his protection over me, blesses me, and covers me with favor as with a shield. (Psalm 5:11-12)

God has turned my mourning into dancing; he has clothed me with gladness. I will give thanks to God forever! (Psalm 30:11-12)

I rejoice in the Lord, because he has clothed me with salvation and covered me with righteousness. (Isaiah 61:10)

I will rejoice and be glad in God's love, because he has seen my affliction; he has known the distress of my soul, and has not delivered me into the hand of the enemy; he has set my feet in a broad place. (Psalm 31:7-8)

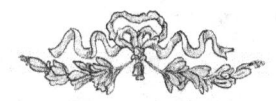

CHAPTER THIRTEEN

PEACE

Last night, I watched *The Sound of Music*. If you haven't seen it, stop everything you're doing and watch it. It's a classic. In one of the scenes, Georg von Trapp's children, scared of the thunderstorm outside, run into Fraulein Maria's bedroom for comfort. Maria tells them, "If anything bugs me and I'm feeling unhappy, I just try and think of nice things!" The children ask, "What kind of things?" and Maria begins to sing about some of her favourite things—raindrops on roses and whiskers on kittens, and a whole lot of other things that make her feel better.

This song has a very biblical principle. Philippians 4:6-8 says,

> *Do not be anxious about anything, but in everything by prayer and supplication with thanksgiving let your requests be made known to God. And the peace of God, which surpasses all understanding, will guard your hearts and your minds in Christ Jesus. Finally, brothers, whatever is true, whatever is honorable, whatever is just, whatever is pure, whatever is lovely,*

> *whatever is commendable, if there is any excellence, if there is anything worthy of praise, think about these things.*

ACTIVATION

I've heard Pastor Creflo Dollar say that worrying is just meditating on the wrong thing. Philippians 4:6-8 offers us a very practical way to experience God's peace, and tells us what to meditate on instead. Begin by giving thanks to God. Then, let your requests be made known to Him. Finally, think about things that are:

- True
- Honorable
- Just
- Pure
- Lovely
- Commendable
- Excellent
- Worthy of praise

GOD'S MIRROR WORDS ABOUT PEACE

Do not be anxious about anything, but in everything by prayer and supplication with thanksgiving let your requests be made known to God. And the peace of God, which surpasses all understanding, will guard your hearts and your minds in Christ Jesus. Finally, brothers, whatever is true, whatever is honorable, whatever is just, whatever is pure, whatever is lovely, whatever is commendable, if there is any excellence, if there is anything worthy of praise, think about these things.

PHILIPPIANS 4:6-8

If then you have been raised with Christ, seek the things that are above, where Christ is, seated at the right hand of God. Set your mind on things that are above, not on things that are on earth. For you have died, and your life is hidden with Christ in God.

COLOSSIANS 3:1-3

You keep him in perfect peace whose mind is stayed on you, because he trusts in you.

ISAIAH 26:3

O Lord, my heart is not lifted up; my eyes are not raised too high; I do not occupy myself with things too great and too marvelous for me. But I have calmed and quieted my soul, like a weaned child with its mother; like a weaned child is my soul within me.

PSALM 131:1-2

When the cares of my heart are many, your consolations cheer my soul.

PSALM 94:19

For though we walk in the flesh, we are not waging war according to the flesh. For the weapons of our warfare are not of the flesh but have divine power to destroy strongholds. We destroy arguments and every lofty opinion raised against the knowledge of God, and take every thought captive to obey Christ.

2 CORINTHIANS 10:3-5

Cast your burden on the Lord, and he will sustain you; he will never permit the righteous to be moved.

PSALM 55:22

"For the mountains may depart and the hills be removed, but my steadfast love shall not depart from you, and my covenant of peace shall not be removed," says the Lord, who has compassion on you.

ISAIAH 54:10

Hear my cry, O God, listen to my prayer; from the end of the earth I call to you when my heart is faint. Lead me to the rock that is higher than I, for you have been my refuge, a strong tower against the enemy. Let me dwell in your tent forever! Let me take refuge under the shadow of your wings! Selah.

PSALM 61:1-4

Be still, and know that I am God. I will be exalted among the nations, I will be exalted in the earth!

PSALM 46:10

Therefore I tell you, do not be anxious about your life, what you will eat or what you will drink, nor about your body, what you will put on. Is not life more than food, and the body more than clothing? Look at the birds of the air: they neither sow nor reap nor gather into barns, and yet your heavenly Father feeds them. Are you not of more value than they? And which of you by being anxious can add a single hour to his span of life? And why are you anxious about clothing? Consider the lilies of the field, how they grow: they neither toil nor spin, yet I tell you, even Solomon in all his glory was not arrayed like one of these. But if God so clothes the grass of the field, which today is alive and tomorrow is thrown into the oven, will he not much more clothe you, O you of little faith? Therefore do not be anxious, saying, 'What shall we eat?' or 'What shall we drink?' or 'What shall we wear?' For the Gentiles seek after all these things, and your heavenly Father knows you need them all. But seek first the kingdom of God and his righteousness, and all these things will be added to you.

MATTHEW 6:25-33

Come to me, all who labor and are heavy laden, and I will give you rest. Take my yoke upon you, and learn from me, for I am gentle and lowly in heart, and you will find rest for your souls. For my yoke is easy, and my burden is light.

MATTHEW 11:28-30

I have said these things to you, that in me you may have peace. In the world you will have tribulation. But take heart; I have overcome the world.

JOHN 16:33

May the Lord give strength to his people! May the Lord bless his people with peace!

PSALM 29:11

Why are you cast down, O my soul, and why are you in turmoil within me? Hope in God; for I shall again praise him, my salvation and my God.

PSALM 42:11

Then they cried to the Lord in their trouble, and he delivered them from their distress. He made the storm be still, and the waves of the sea were hushed. Then they were glad that the waters were quiet, and he brought them to their desired haven.

PSALM 107:28-30

And he awoke and rebuked the wind and said to the sea, "Peace! Be still!" And the wind ceased, and there was a great calm.

MARK 4:39

Peace I leave with you; my peace I give to you. Not as the world gives do I give to you. Let not your hearts be troubled, neither let them be afraid.

JOHN 14:27

In peace I will both lie down and sleep; for you alone, O Lord, make me dwell in safety.

PSALM 4:8

I Declare:

God keeps me in perfect peace because my mind is stayed on him, because I trust in him. (Isaiah 26:3)

I will not let my heart be troubled, I will not be afraid. (John 14:27)

I am not anxious about anything, but in everything by prayer and supplication with thanksgiving I let my requests be known to God. And the peace of God, which surpasses all understanding, guards my heart and mind in Christ Jesus. I only think about things that are true, honorable, just, pure, lovely, commendable, excellent, and worthy of praise. (Philippians 4:6-8)

Because I have been raised with Christ, I seek the things that are above, where Christ is, seated at the right hand of God. I set my mind on things that are above, not on things that are on earth. Because I have died, and my life is hidden with Christ in God. (Colossians 3:1-3)

I seek first the kingdom of God and his righteousness, and everything I need is added to me. (Matthew 6:25-33)

I cast my burden on the Lord, and he sustains me; he will never let me be moved. (Psalm 55:22)

God's steadfast love will never leave me, and his covenant of peace will not be removed. (Isaiah 54:10)

I take every thought captive to obey Christ. (2 Corinthians 10:3-5)

God's yoke is easy, and his burden is light. (Matthew 11:28-30)

When the cares of my heart are many, God's consolations cheer my soul. (Psalm 94:19)

God is my refuge and strong tower against the enemy. (Psalm 61:1-4)

In peace I will both lie down and sleep; for you alone, O Lord, make me dwell in safety. (Psalm 4:8)

CHAPTER FOURTEEN
FEARLESSNESS

11 November 2019

What makes me unblock him?

Fear that he will move on and find someone that makes him happier, while I'm alone and still single. The truth is — God will never tell me to walk away from someone or something without having something better.

Fear that he and his friends will compare his future girl with me. The truth is — that's his problem. Instead of my former shame I shall have a twofold recompense. I will possess double what I forfeited. Everlasting joy shall be mine (Isaiah 61:7). God is preparing a table for me in the presence of my enemies (Psalm 23:5).

Fear that he will be a better man to his next, prettier, girl. The truth is — the prudent man sees the evil and hides himself.

> But the simple pass on and are punished with suffering (Proverbs 22:3). I want someone honest, not someone that knows just what to say to get into any girl's pants. Honesty and character take time to build. If God is telling me to walk away, it's likely he's not going to change any time soon.

A few nights ago, I dreamt about what I fear the most. I won't go into what happened in the dream, but as I was waking up I said, "Good morning, Holy Spirit. Good morning, Father. Good morning, Jesus." I immediately felt God say, "Fear is partnering with the devil. Faith is partnering with Me." I was reminded of Isaiah 54:14 which says: "In righteousness you shall be established; you shall be far from oppression, for you shall not fear; and from terror, for it shall not come near you."

This verse doesn't say that you shall be far from fear, for you shall not be oppressed. It says that you shall be far from oppression, for you shall not fear. Fear is partnering with the devil, meditating on his plans for your life. It is meditating on destruction (John 10:10). Faith is partnering with God, meditating on His plans for your life. It is meditating on righteousness, peace and joy (Romans 14:17).

That morning I felt God say, "Don't partner with the devil. Give no room to him. Fear not. I am with you. Do you know what it means for Me to be with you? I hold your right hand. I lead and guide you. Nothing can separate you from My love. Be bold and courageous."

COMMUNITY

1 John 4:18 says:

> *There is no fear in love, but perfect love casts out fear. For fear has to do with punishment, and whoever fears*

> has not been perfected in love.

If perfect love casts out fear, and whoever fears has not been perfected in love, how do we become perfected in love? Let's read the previous few verses.

> No one has ever seen God; if we love one another, God abides in us and His love is perfected in us (v 12).

If perfect love casts out fear, and God's love is perfected in us when we love one another, we need community in order to be fearless. It took me nearly a year to break free from my relationship with my ex. I had an intimate relationship with God, but I didn't have community with others. It wasn't until I started bible college, and made friendships with people who called out 'the gold' in me each week, that I really started to see my worth and find the strength I needed to stop going back to my ex.

In the first chapter I mentioned that it is extremely hard to break free from an abusive relationship without having anything or anyone better to cling to. I shared how intimacy with God is the most important tool to aid your healing. In this section, I want to highlight what I believe is the second most important tool you will need in your healing journey: being in community with others. You may have lost friendships during your relationship, or isolated yourself because of it, but I want to encourage you to pray and make declarations about the kind of friendships you want in your life.

Ecclesiastes 4:9–12 says,

> Two are better than one, because they have a good reward for their toil. For if they fall, one will lift up his fellow. But woe to him who is alone when he falls and has not another to lift him up! Again, if two lie together, they keep warm, but how can one keep warm alone?

> *And though a man might prevail against one who is alone, two will withstand him—a threefold cord is not quickly broken.*

Here's an example of the declarations I made about the kind of friendships I wanted in my life:

- God has given me lots of fun, adventurous, caring Christian friends who love Jesus and love me.

- People are drawn to me.

- I have a solid group of close friends that I go on adventures with, travel with, pray with, worship with, and evangelise with. We have lots of fun and laughs.

- I have a great social life. I am never bored or lonely.

Bear in mind, when I was making these declarations, I was lonely. I had lost friendships with people who were frustrated with me going back to my ex. But our words are powerful, and God gave me what I declared. I no longer felt the need to jump into another relationship because of the love I received from God, and the friends He placed in my life.

ACTIVATION

If you are hungry for friendship like I was, pray and make declarations about the friendships you want in your life. Add works to your faith by involving yourself in church and Young Adults events if you are a young adult. Be friendly, be yourself, and let it happen.

God's Mirror Words About Fearlessness

God gave us a spirit not of fear but of power and love and self-control.

2 TIMOTHY 1:7

Be strong and courageous. Do not fear or be in dread of them, for it is the Lord your God who goes with you. He will not leave you or forsake you.

DEUTERONOMY 31:6

Have I not commanded you? Be strong and courageous. Do not be frightened, and do not be dismayed, for the Lord your God is with you wherever you go.

JOSHUA 1:9

But now thus says the Lord, he who created you, O Jacob, he who formed you, O Israel: "Fear not, for I have redeemed you; I have called you by name, you are mine. When you pass through the waters, I will be with you; and through the rivers, they shall not overwhelm you; when you walk through fire you shall not be burned, and the flame shall not consume you."

ISAIAH 43:1-2

Even though I walk through the valley of the shadow of death, I will fear no evil, for you are with me; your rod and your staff, they comfort me.

PSALM 23:4

Be sober-minded; be watchful. Your adversary the devil prowls around like a roaring lion, seeking someone to devour. Resist him, firm in your faith, knowing that the same kinds of suffering are being experienced by your brotherhood throughout the world. And after you have suffered a little while, the God of all grace, who has called you to his eternal glory in Christ, will himself restore, confirm, strengthen, and establish you.

I PETER 5:8-10

Fear not, for you will not be ashamed; be not confounded, for you will not be disgraced; for you will forget the shame of your youth, and the reproach of your widowhood you will remember no more.

ISAIAH 54:4

Those who look to him are radiant, and their faces shall never be ashamed.

PSALM 34:5

He gives power to the faint, and to him who has no might he increases strength. Even youths shall faint and be weary, and young men shall fall exhausted; but they who wait for the Lord shall renew their strength; they shall mount up with wings like eagles; they shall run and not be weary; they shall walk and not faint.

ISAIAH 40:29-31

Fear not, for I am with you; be not dismayed, for I am your God; I will strengthen you, I will help you, I will uphold you with my righteous right hand.

ISAIAH 41:10

I have set the Lord always before me; because he is at my right hand, I shall not be shaken. Therefore my heart is glad, and my whole being rejoices; my flesh also dwells secure. For you will not abandon my soul to Sheol, or let your holy one see corruption.

PSALM 16:8-10

I can do all things through him who strengthens me.

PHILIPPIANS 4:13

For by you I can run against a troop, and by my God I can leap over a wall.

PSALM 18:29

For everyone who has been born of God overcomes the world. And this is the victory that has overcome the world – our faith. Who is it that overcomes the world except the one who believes that Jesus is the Son of God?

1 JOHN 5:4-5

Be strong, and let your heart take courage, all you who wait for the Lord!

PSALM 31:24

Lie not in wait as a wicked man against the dwelling of the righteous; do no violence to his home; for the righteous falls seven times and rises again, but the wicked stumble in times of calamity.

PROVERBS 24:15-16

> *The angel of the Lord encamps around those who fear him, and delivers them.*
>
> PSALM 34:7

> *I sought the Lord, and he answered me and delivered me from all my fears.*
>
> PSALM 34:4

> *Many are the afflictions of the righteous, but the Lord delivers him out of them all.*
>
> PSALM 34:19

> *The name of the Lord is a strong tower; the righteous man runs into it and is safe.*
>
> PROVERBS 18:10

> *The Lord is a stronghold for the oppressed, a stronghold in times of trouble. And those who know your name put their trust in you, for you, O Lord, have not forsaken those who seek you.*
>
> PSALM 9:9-10

Mark the blameless and behold the upright, for there is a future for the man of peace. But transgressors shall be altogether destroyed; the future of the wicked shall be cut off. The salvation of the righteous is from the Lord; he is their stronghold in the time of trouble. The Lord helps them and delivers them; he delivers them from the wicked and saves them, because they take refuge in him.

PSALM 37:37-40

I Declare:

God has not given me a spirit of fear but of power and love and self-control. (2 Timothy 1:7)

I am strong and courageous. God will not leave me or forsake me. He is with me wherever I go. (Deuteronomy 31:6; Joshua 1:9)

God has redeemed me; he has called me by name, I am his. When I pass through the waters, God will be with me; and through the rivers, they will not overwhelm me; when I walk through fire I will not be burned, and the flame will not consume me. (Isaiah 43:1-2)

I will fear no evil because God is with me and he comforts me. (Psalm 23:4)

I will not be ashamed; I will not be disgraced; I will forget the shame of my youth. (Isaiah 54:4)

I look to God and am radiant, my face will never be ashamed. (Psalm 34:5)

Because I wait for the Lord I will renew my strength; I will mount up with wings like eagles; I will run and not be weary; I will walk and not faint. (Isaiah 40:29-31)

God will strengthen me, help me, and uphold me with his righteous right hand. (Isaiah 41:10)

Because God is at my right hand, I will not be shaken. My heart is glad, my whole being rejoices; my flesh dwells secure. God will not abandon my soul or let me see corruption. (Psalm 16:8-10)

I can do all things through Christ who strengthens me. (Philippians 4:13)

Everyone who has been born of God overcomes the world. Therefore I overcome the world. (1 John 5:4-5)

The angel of the Lord encamps around me, and delivers me. (Psalm 34:7)

The righteous falls seven times and rises again. (Proverbs 24:15-16)

The Lord delivers me from all my fears and afflictions. (Psalm 34:4; Psalm 34:19)

The name of the Lord is a strong tower, I run into it and am safe. (Proverbs 18:10)

CHAPTER FIFTEEN
PURPOSE

In 2012, while I was praying about what God had called me to do, God gave me the same dream three nights in a row. In the dream, there were men standing on one side of my street, and women on the other. The women started running away from the men, and I was at the front, leading them with a couple of other women. We lead them to a safe place underground and gave them clothes out of giant clothing bins. I had no idea what this dream meant at the time, but I started feeling extremely sensitive whenever I saw or heard anything to do with violence against women.

I ended up swapping out of my business degree course to study psychology and social work. Halfway through my Master of Social Work degree, I figured it was time to look for a social work-related job. I applied for a lot of different jobs, and went to three different interviews, only to get rejected by them all. After about six months of searching, I finally got offered a position with a domestic violence organisation, assisting women fleeing domestic violence to get into safe accommodation in women's shelters. The job perfectly aligned with the dream I had all those years ago!

What's the point in all of this? Only that *rejection is often God's redirection.* The three job interviews I went for included a women's hostel, a youth organisation, and a homelessness service. They all would have been beautiful jobs, and they were all social work-related, but they weren't aligned with what God had called **me** to do.

Your value doesn't come from who's texting you or who isn't texting you, or who is employing you or not! Your value does not change because of your relationship or status. You are just as valuable whether you're alone or not alone. Shift your perspective today. When you face rejection of any kind, rejoice that God has protected you!

28 January 2020

> I'm not withholding anything good from you. The only thing I'm withholding is a lot of pain, trauma, abuse, neglect, lies, heartache, deterioration of self-esteem and mental health.

No one will be enough for a man who isn't enough for himself. You will never be loved properly by someone who doesn't love themselves. And people cannot truly love themselves unless they know God and have a revelation of the deep, unfailing love that He has for them.

Losing someone that doesn't love, respect, and value you is actually a gain not a loss. What have you gained by losing your ex? You have gained a peace of mind. You have gained a confidence that cannot be shaken, because God has drawn you back to Himself and reminded you of who you are. You have gained a new type of waiting; instead of waiting for the wrong person to change, you are waiting for God to lead you to the right person. But not just that. You have learned that it is only God that can truly satisfy you, make you joyful (a joy that does not depend on what has or has not happened), make you whole. Your confidence, security, and worth come from Christ alone.

God brings diamonds out of tough situations and pain. Diamonds that would not have been there otherwise. God can heal your broken heart so well that you are more beautiful as a result of what has happened than you would have been had it not have happened at all!

ACTIVATION

This doesn't have to be a sad time. In His presence there is fullness of joy (Psalm 16:11). Your mission, should you choose to accept it, is to have a praise party in your room for all God has protected you from! Put on "Love on Fire" by Bethel Music and dance like no one's watching.

God's Mirror Words About Purpose

For my thoughts are not your thoughts, neither are your ways my ways, declares the Lord. For as the heavens are higher than the earth, so are my ways higher than your ways and my thoughts than your thoughts.

ISAIAH 55:8-9

The steps of a man are established by the Lord, when he delights in his way; though he fall, he shall not be cast headlong, for the Lord upholds his hand.

PSALM 37:23-24

The heart of man plans his way, but the Lord establishes his steps.

PROVERBS 16:9

Many are the plans in the mind of a man, but it is the purpose of the Lord that will stand.

PROVERBS 19:21

And your ears shall hear a word behind you, saying, "This is the way, walk in it," when you turn to the right or when you turn to the left.

ISAIAH 30:21

For the moment all discipline seems painful rather than pleasant, but later it yields the peaceful fruit of righteousness to those who have been trained by it.

HEBREWS 12:11

And Samuel said, "Has the Lord as great delight in burnt offerings and sacrifices, as in obeying the voice of the Lord? Behold, to obey is better than sacrifice, and to listen than the fat of rams.

I SAMUEL 15:22

Unless the Lord builds the house, those who build it labor in vain. Unless the Lord watches over the city, the watchman stays awake in vain.

PSALM 127:1

Therefore , since we are surrounded by so great a cloud of witnesses, let us also lay aside every weight, and sin which clings so closely, and let us run with endurance the race that is set before us, looking to Jesus, the founder and perfecter of our faith, who for the joy that was set before him endured the cross, despising the shame, and is seated at the right hand of the throne of God.

HEBREWS 12:1-2

God is not man, that he should lie, or a son of man, that he should change his mind. Has he said, and will he not do it? Or has he spoken, and will he not fulfill it?

NUMBERS 23:19

I perceived that whatever God does endures forever; nothing can be added to it, nor anything taken from it. God has done it, so that people fear before him.

ECCLESIASTES 3:14

For I know the plans I have for you, declares the Lord, plans for welfare and not for evil, to give you a future and a hope.

JEREMIAH 29:11

For all the promises of God find their Yes in him. That is why it is through him that we utter our Amen to God for his glory.

2 CORINTHIANS 1:20

I Declare:

God's ways are higher than my ways and his thoughts are higher than my thoughts. (Isaiah 55:8-9)

My steps are established by the Lord. (Psalm 37:23-24; Proverbs 19:21)

I hear God's voice and obey him. (Isaiah 30:21; 1 Samuel 15:22)

God's plans for me are plans for welfare and not for evil, to give me a future and a hope. (Jeremiah 29:11)

I lay aside every weight, and run with endurance the race that is set before me, looking to Jesus who is seated at the right hand of God. (Hebrews 12:1-2)

God is not man, that he should lie, or a son of man, that he should change his mind. He will do what he said he will do. (Numbers 23:19)

CHAPTER SIXTEEN
WISDOM

There is wisdom in letting go of people who are harmful toward your mental or physical health. The day after my ex and I broke up (for the final time), my friends Shu and Andre video-called me. They had no idea what I was going through. They just felt strongly prompted by the Holy Spirit to contact me. They spent an hour talking to me about their story, their individual seasons of singleness, and their marriage. Then, Andre spoke to me about forgiveness. He told me that forgiveness doesn't mean going back to the mud puddle. "If someone hits me on the head with a stick, I can forgive them and release them, but does that mean that I go back to them to get hit with the stick again? No way!" Andre explained that loyalty doesn't mean staying in the mud puddle. He told me that I only needed to be loyal to God.

While forgiveness is essential to your healing, it does not mean that you take your healed heart back to the person that broke it. You are not a dog that returns to his vomit (Proverbs 26:11). Even the most violent and abusive relationships have happy moments. But you can't hold onto something that crushes your spirit. I love what Pastor Creflo Dollar says: "If it costs you your peace, it's too expensive."

15 April 2020

Lord, why am I struggling to let go?
You're still waiting for him to change. The thing is, I'm still waiting for him to change too. I have no control over if or when he surrenders his life to Me. I have revealed Myself to him a number of times, even through you, and I will continue to reveal Myself to him. But everyone has a choice.

They say it takes an average of six to nine attempts to leave an abusive relationship before leaving the relationship permanently. If you're anything like I was, and have gone back to your ex a thousand times, don't beat yourself up. God doesn't see you as a bad person or as weak. He wants you to see yourself the way He sees you. Don't let what happened distance you from Him. He understands what you're going through and He wants to walk through it with you.

ACTIVATION

Pastor Creflo Dollar says, "If it costs you your peace it's too expensive." Your challenge today is to unfollow, delete, or block, anyone or anything on social media that is costing you your peace.

GOD'S MIRROR WORDS ABOUT WISDOM

Keep your heart with all diligence, for out of it spring the issues of life.

PROVERBS 4:23 (NKJV)

Trusting in a treacherous man in time of trouble is like a bad tooth or a foot that slips.

PROVERBS 25:19

For you may be sure of this, that everyone who is sexually immoral or impure, or who is covetous (that is, an idolater) has no inheritance in the kingdom of Christ and God. Let no one deceive you with empty words, for because of these things the wrath of God comes upon the sons of disobedience. Therefore do not become partners with them; for at one time you were darkness, but now you are light in the Lord. Walk as children of light.

EPHESIANS 5:5-8

No temptation has overtaken you that is not common to man. God is faithful, and he will not let you be tempted beyond your ability, but with the temptation he will also provide the way of escape, that you may be able to endure it.

I CORINTHIANS 10:13

Turn my eyes from looking at worthless things; and give me life in your ways.

PSALM 119:37

Whoever restrains his words has knowledge, and he who has a cool spirit is a man of understanding. Even a fool who keeps silent is considered wise; when he closes his lips, he is deemed intelligent.

PROVERBS 17:27-28

It is an honor for a man to keep aloof from strife, but every fool will be quarreling.

PROVERBS 20:3

Whoever guards his mouth preserves his life; he who opens wide his lips comes to ruin.

PROVERBS 13:3

Whoever guards his mouth and tongue keeps his soul from troubles.

PROVERBS 21:23 (NKJV)

From the fruit of a man's mouth his stomach is satisfied; he is satisfied by the yield of his lips. Death and life are in the power of the tongue, and those who love it will eat its fruits.

PROVERBS 18:20-21

One who is full loathes honey, but to one who is hungry everything bitter is sweet.

PROVERBS 27:7

Anxiety in a man's heart weighs him down, but a good word makes him glad.

PROVERBS 12:25

Oil and perfume make the heart glad, and the sweetness of a friend comes from his earnest counsel.

PROVERBS 27:9

Faithful are the wounds of a friend, but the kisses of an enemy are deceitful.

PROVERBS 27:6 (NKJV)

Whoever ignores instruction despises himself, but he who listens to reproof gains intelligence.

PROVERBS 15:32

A fool despises his father's instruction, but whoever receives correction is prudent.

PROVERBS 15:5 (NKJV)

A wise man is full of strength, and a man of knowledge enhances his might, for by wise guidance you can wage your war, and in abundance of counselors there is victory.

PROVERBS 24:5-6

Where there is no guidance, a people falls, but in an abundance of counselors there is safety.

PROVERBS 11:14

By pride comes nothing but strife, but with the well-advised is wisdom.

PROVERBS 13:10 (NKJV)

You will recognize them by their fruits. Are grapes gathered from thornbushes, or figs from thistles? So, every healthy tree bears good fruit, but the diseased tree bears bad fruit. A healthy tree cannot bear bad fruit, nor can a diseased tree bear good fruit. Every tree that does not bear good fruit is cut down and thrown into the fire. Thus you will recognize them by their fruits.

MATTHEW 7:16-20

Either make the tree good and its fruit good, or make the tree bad and its fruit bad, for the tree is known by its fruit. You brood of vipers! How can you speak good, when you are evil? For out of the abundance of the heart the mouth speaks. The good person out of his good treasure brings forth good, and the evil person out of his evil treasure brings forth evil.

MATTHEW 12:33-35

Even a child makes himself known by his acts, by whether his conduct is pure and upright.

PROVERBS 20:11

But the Lord said to Samuel, "Do not look on his appearance or on the height of his stature, because I have rejected him. For the Lord sees not as man sees: man looks on the outward appearance, but the Lord looks on the heart."

I SAMUEL 16:7

Truthful lips endure forever, but a lying tongue is but for a moment.

PROVERBS 12:19

I charge you, O daughters of Jerusalem, do not stir up nor awaken love until it pleases.

SONG OF SOLOMON 8:4 (NKJV)

A man without self-control is like a city broken into and left without walls.

PROVERBS 25:28

Look carefully then how you walk, not as unwise but as wise, making the best use of the time, because the days are evil. Therefore do not be foolish, but understand what the will of the Lord is.

EPHESIANS 5:15-17

The prudent sees danger and hides himself, but the simple go on and suffer for it.

PROVERBS 22:3

The simple believes everything, but the prudent gives thought to his steps.

PROVERBS 14:15

Like a dog that returns to his vomit is a fool who repeats his folly.

PROVERBS 26:11

The fear of the Lord leads to life, and whoever has it rests satisfied; he will not be visited by harm.

PROVERBS 19:23

Everyone then who hears these words of mine and does them will be like a wise man who built his house on the rock. And the rain fell, and the floods came, and the winds blew and beat on that house, but it did not fall, because it had been founded on the rock. And everyone who hears these words of mine and does not do them will be like a foolish man who built his house on the sand. And the rain fell, and the floods came, and the winds blew and beat against that house, and it fell, and great was the fall of it.

MATTHEW 7:24-27

I Declare:

I guard my heart with all vigilance. (Proverbs 4:23)

I do not let anyone deceive me with empty words. (Ephesians 5:5-8)

God is faithful, and he will not let me be tempted beyond my ability, but with the temptation he will also provide the way of escape, so that I can endure it. (1 Corinthians 10:13)

I do not look at worthless things. (Psalm 119:37)

Because I have knowledge and understanding, I restrain my words and have a calm spirit. (Proverbs 17:27-28)

Death and life are in the power of my tongue, so I use my words to speak life. (Proverbs 18:20-21)

In Christ I am fully satisfied, so nothing bitter is sweet to me. (Proverbs 27:7)

I am strong and safe because I am surrounded by an abundance of wise counselors. (Proverbs 24:5-6; Proverbs 11:14; Proverbs 13:10)

I will not stir up or awaken love until it pleases. (Song of Solomon 8:4)

I am prudent, wise, and make the best use of time because I understand what God's will is. (Ephesians 5:15-17; Proverbs 22:3; Proverbs 14:15)

I am not a dog that returns to his vomit. I will not take my healing back to what hurt me. (Proverbs 26:11)

I obey God's word and voice. (Matthew 7:24-27)

Because I have the fear of the Lord, I rest satisfied; I will not be visited by harm. (Proverbs 19:23)

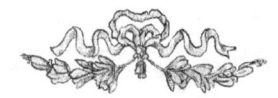

CHAPTER SEVENTEEN

TRUST

19 September 2019

If only you could see what I have in store for you.

It would have been a lot easier to let go of my ex if Jesus knocked on my door and showed me a picture of me ten years from now with my six-foot tall husband, three babies, and investment property. It's easy to trust that the seat we are sitting on won't break, but when it comes to trusting God with our future it's not so straightforward. We fear He will either keep us single for the rest of our lives, or force us to marry someone we aren't attracted to. But God gives good gifts to His children. Matthew 7:11 says, "If you then, who are evil, know how to give good gifts to your children, how much more will your Father who is in heaven give good things to those who ask him!"

God only wants the best for His children. He knows the desires of your heart. Don't let your age or societal pressures lower your standards. This new season is going to be incredible. You need to let go of the old to take hold of the new. You can let go. It's going to be okay.

There is nothing 'wrong' with you. You don't need to be more of this or less of that. You just need to trust God and trust His timing, and He will give you the grace to do that. Also, God's not going to make you marry someone you're not attracted to! Remember that story I told you about my job? I believe it will be the same with the person we end up with. He's going to be a better fit for us than all the jobs we applied for, and all the interviews we went to. God's timing is perfect.

No break ups are easy. Right now, maybe it hurts. It doesn't always feel great. But you are in God's will when you submit to Him. God's will is the best place you can be—the safest, most fun, most fulfilling. You will get the most out of your life when you submit to His will. Just wait. He will blow your mind.

This heartbreak, anger, pain, disappointment, betrayal—it is not going to end this way. You are not going to stay broken, bitter, weak, or hurt. You are not going to stay single for the rest of your life. This heartbreak is going to be used to honour God and promote His glory. Psalm 34:5 says, "Those who look to Him are radiant, and their faces shall never be ashamed." If you look to Him, you will be radiant, and you will never be ashamed.

14 December 2019

Why do I keep going back?

You're afraid you're not going to meet someone else. But when have I ever closed a door and not given you something better? Trust Me and trust My timing. There is nothing wrong with you. Trust Me. Lean back, rest, and enjoy. In My presence there is fullness of joy.

Why do we worry? Because we are not in control. We don't know what the future holds. But we can lean into the promises of God knowing that His plans are good (Jeremiah 29:11), His ways and His thoughts are higher than ours (Isaiah 55:9), He is working all things together for good (Romans 8:28), He is with us, He will not let us down, and He will not abandon us (Deuteronomy 31:8). Therefore, we can be strong and courageous (Joshua 1:9).

ACTIVATION

The word 'cast' means to throw out, down, or away. Psalm 55:22 says:

> *Cast your burden on the Lord, and He will sustain you; He will never permit the righteous to be moved.*

1 Peter 5:7 says:

> *Casting all your anxieties on Him, because He cares for you.*

Put your hand out in front of you. Imagine all your anxieties, all your cares, all your worries in your hand. Now, throw them to God.

Still thinking about them? Write them out in a journal entry to God. There's something therapeutic about getting your thoughts out of your head and onto paper.

God's Mirror Words About Trust

Trust in the Lord with all your heart, and do not lean on your own understanding. In all your ways acknowledge him, and he will make straight your paths.

PROVERBS 3:5-6

The Lord will fulfill his purpose for me; your steadfast love, O Lord, endures forever. Do not forsake the work of your hands.

PSALM 138:8

Commit your way to the Lord; trust in him, and he will act. He will bring forth your righteousness as the light, and your justice as the noonday. Be still before the Lord and wait patiently for him; fret not yourself over the one who prospers in his way, over the man who carries out evil devices!

PSALM 37:5-7

Whoever gives thought to the word will discover good, and blessed is he who trusts in the Lord.

PROVERBS 16:20

The fear of man lays a snare, but whoever trusts in the Lord is safe.

PROVERBS 29:25

When I am afraid, I put my trust in you.

PSALM 56:3

Thus says the Lord: "Cursed is the man who trusts in man and makes flesh his strength, whose heart turns away from the Lord. He is like a shrub in the desert, and shall not see any good come. He shall dwell in the parched places of the wilderness, and in an uninhabited salt land. Blessed is the man who trusts in the Lord, whose trust is in the Lord. He is like a tree planted by water, that sends out its roots by the stream, and does not fear when heat comes, for its leaves remain green, and is not anxious in the year of drought, for it does not cease to bear fruit."

JEREMIAH 17:5-8

Now I know that the Lord saves his anointed; he will answer him from his holy heaven with the saving might of his right hand. Some trust in chariots and some in horses, but we trust in the name of the Lord our God.

PSALM 20:6-7

This God – his way is perfect; the word of the Lord proves true; he is a shield for all those who take refuge in him.

PSALM 18:30

I believe that I shall look upon the goodness of the Lord in the land of the living! Wait for the Lord; be strong, and let your heart take courage; wait for the Lord!

PSALM 27:13-14

For still the vision awaits its appointed time; it hastens to the end – it will not lie. If it seems slow, wait for it; it will surely come; it will not delay.

HABAKKUK 2:3

For everything there is a season, and a time for every matter under heaven: a time to be born, and a time to die; a time to plant, and a time to pluck up what is planted; a time to kill, and a time to heal; a time to break down, and a time to build up; a time to weep, and a time to laugh; a time to mourn, and a time to dance; a time to cast away stones, and a time to gather stones together; a time to embrace, and a time to refrain from embracing; a time to seek, and a time to lose; a time to keep, and a time to cast away; a time to tear, and a time to sew; a time to keep silence, and a time to speak; a time to love, and a time to hate; a time for war, and a time for peace.

ECCLESIASTES 3:1-8

He has made everything beautiful in its time. Also, he has put eternity into man's heart, yet so that he cannot find out what God has done from the beginning to the end.

ECCLESIASTES 3:11

I Declare:

I trust in the Lord with all my heart, and do not lean on my own understanding. In all my ways I acknowledge him, and he makes my paths straight. (Proverbs 3:5-6)

The Lord will fulfill his purpose for me. He will not forsake the work of his hands. (Psalm 138:8)

The Lord brings forth my righteousness as the light, and my justice as the noonday. (Psalm 37:5-7)

I am blessed because my trust is in the Lord, not in man. (Jeremiah 17:5 -8; Proverbs 29:25)

God's way is perfect; his word proves true. (Psalm 18:30)

When I am afraid, I put my trust in God. (Psalm 56:3)

I believe that I will see the goodness of the Lord in the land of the living! I am strong and courageous. I will wait for the Lord! (Psalm 27:13-14)

CONCLUSION

In the end we all have a choice. We can choose to look at the mirror of social media, our ex, and what other people think, to tell us who we are. Or, we can choose to look at the words of life, the words of truth. It's knowing the truth that will set us free (John 8:32).

If I could add any word of encouragement, it would be to:

1. Focus on intimacy with the Father
2. Pray for community; and
3. Remember who you are

When you know your worth, it will be impossible to settle for cheap love. I'm praying for you.

With lots of love,

Ruth Augustine

P.S. If you're wondering what happened to the princess in the story, she got rid of the mirror Prince Charming gave her and lived happily ever after with her father who gave her the words of life.

www.ingramcontent.com/pod-product-compliance
Lightning Source LLC
Chambersburg PA
CBHW051439290426
44109CB00016B/1618